# threadwork

## silks, stitches, beads & cords

*Dedicated to the creative spirit in all of us,*
*to my sister Myrtle and my daughters Helen and Maria*

First published in 2009 by
Sally Milner Publishing Pty Ltd
734 Woodville Road
Binda NSW 2583 AUSTRALIA

© Effie Mitrofanis 2009

Design: Caroline Verity
Editing: Anne Savage
Photography: Lee Sincic
Illustrations: Anna Warren

Printed in China
National Library of Australia Cataloguing-in-Publication data:
    Author: Mitofanis, Effie
    Title: Threadwork : silks, stitches, beads and cords / Effie Mitofanis
    ISBN: 9781863514033 (pbk.)
    Series: Milner craft series
    Notes: Includes index
    Subjects: Embroidery--Technique; Embroidery--Patterns
    Dewey Number: 46.44

**Disclaimer**

*Information and instructions given in this book are presented in good faith, but no warranty is given nor results guaranteed,
nor is freedom from any patent to be inferred. As we have no control over physical conditions surrounding application of
information herein contained in this book, the author and publisher disclaim any liability for untoward results.*

10 9 8 7 6 5 4 3 2 1

# threadwork
## silks, stitches, beads & cords

### Effie Mitrofanis

SALLYMILNER
PUBLISHING

# contents

## acknowledgements

My sister Myrtle, who cared for me when I was ill, for her encouragement and moral support and for helping me make 160 cocoons.

Katha Jones, kinesiologist, for bringing me to good health.

Mladen Ivosevic, Professor of Fine Arts, for his course 'A Picture of my Soul'.

Deena Thompson, for her very special friendship and discernment.

Dr Danny Chow, for stitching me up.

Jan Smith, Iyengar Yoga teacher.

Eileen Gale, who introduced me to creative embroidery and checks my home while I'm away teaching.

Jan Hartley, my Reiki partner, for being there.

Jessie Hosie, for her support and helping me make cocoons.

Jack Joynes, for taking initial photos of step-by-step instructions.

Joan Jeffriess, for her tip on 'bagging'.

Wendy and Ron Schmidt, for encouragement and support.

Lee Sincic, photographer and teacher extraordinaire—our fifth book together.

Anne Savage, the best editor anyone could have—our fourth book together.

Anna Warren, talented and versatile graphic artist, and Caroline Verity for her creative book design.

Libby Renney, Publishing Director, Sally Milner Publishing Pty Ltd, for her encouragement and bringing this all together.

I am grateful to the following sponsors: Colour Streams (Robyn Alexander), Leutenegger Pty Ltd, Ristal and Ételage.

# overview

Now that the book is finished I see the resources that have intuitively separated and come forward, to make the connecting threads that stitch this book together, the starting point being beautifully coloured silks, butterflies and patterns of embroidery stitches.

Butterflies, signifying regeneration and rebirth and 'angels in disguise' started to obsess me after I read that 'a butterfly is a moth in an embroidered coat', and was reminded of the many years as a child when I kept silkworms because I loved watching the cycle and waiting to see the different colours of the cocoons from white through to golden yellow, sometimes green.

A butterfly emerges from the egg as a ground-hugging multi-pedal grub that metamorphoses into a silent and dormant state as a chrysalis (from the Greek khrusos, 'gold') within a cocoon (a protective covering). It emerges from this as a two-winged flying apparition whose purpose is to fly around the garden looking beautiful and pollinating plants, then laying eggs for the next cycle.

The way I create at present has evolved over a very long period of studying the history of art and embroidery, making and teaching traditional embroidery techniques and designs and translating them into colourful abstract expressions. I learnt a lot by liking the 'mistakes' I made, breaking the 'rules' and doing the opposite to what I was told and discovering there are many shades of grey between the black and white dogma of how and what is 'the right way'.

A textile tour to China in 1993 strengthened my love of silk and another textile tour to India in 1995 relaxed my previous relatively 'stiff and structured' approach, consciously allowing me to be playful and my embroidery to flow intuitively. I started to experiment and combine what I had previously thought of as 'strange' colour combinations.

I have always been fascinated with three-dimensional texture from ancient stumpwork and the low-relief techniques of an early twentieth century style of embroidery from Casalguidi in Tuscany, Italy, from which my continuous cords evolved.

Wrapped cords developed out of the necessity of making hair braids for a thread promotion and beads and knots and tassels added to them when I had to come up with a new idea every week for a series of classes given to a group of experienced and thirsty craftswomen.

Embroidery transforms and metamorphoses cloth and I now passionately practice and enjoy the process of designing and making with a sense of play using bright colours and beautiful silks.

# introduction

This is a book about creating sumptuous embellished surfaces made by:

***collaging*** rich colourful silks, transparent organza and ribbons,

***stitching*** with embroidery threads and ribbons, knitting and other yarns, and

***adding further texture*** with raised embroidery, cords, metallic threads and beads.

Experience a process of creating where each application allows the surface to evolve from the first layer upwards with a sense of playfulness and thinking outside the square.

Although this may at first appear daunting the process is quite structured as are the instructions for guiding you to achieve your own unique translation.

Although I have given full instructions for all the projects, I encourage you to make variations to the designs or the materials, colours and stitches by using what is available or what you already have, and by relying on your own taste and intuition. Bits and pieces of fabric may be added as the work progresses, as more stitches cover the surface and the embroidery evolves and changes direction as mood and intuition direct.

The method or process is to create an original soft textile by assembling layers of fabric as a background that is embellished with stitches, quilting, beads and cords. The background itself is made from layers of fabrics, starting with a foundation (first layer lining) of two or more layers of openweave lightweight Indian muslin, not calico or homespun. Then a second layer is made by cutting and laying strips and shapes of cut or torn silk, organza and ribbons onto the first layer. After assembling the background, flat stitches are added either before or after embellishment (which is the third layer), to create a subtle, distinctive play of shadows reminiscent of a watercolour wash.

The next step is to build up the surface of the background collage with stitches, exploring their pattern, texture, rhythm and movement using threads of different thicknesses, colour and tonal value, texture and sheen. Individual embroiderer's results will vary depending on the size of the stitches, the tension and spaces between them.

Subsequent layers are created by the use of metallic threads of all kinds for rich and vibrant features, bead and stitch patterns, and cords decorated with patterns of stitches and beads.

Instructions for all the techniques and methods are given in the form of projects so that attractive articles are created while techniques and methods are learned

and explored. A fascinating aspect of this process is that a small project may be enlarged by attaching it to a new lining fabric and repeating the process around the initial piece.

A feature of this method is the impact made by the edges of the fabric pieces. As the project progresses more edges may be added to enrich the surface by applying 'patches' or strips of silk or organza.

Possibilities are given for finishing the final edges of the work—raw and fringed, folded, corded, insertion stitch, ties, beaded and bagged. Discarded selvedges of silk and organza fabrics are also exciting to use in the mix to provide contrasting 'hard' edges.

*Experience a process of creating where each application allows the surface to evolve from the first layer upwards with a sense of playfulness and thinking outside the square.*

Traditionally, embroiderers have been concerned with the negative impact of frayed and raw fabric edges because of laundering constraints—but the positive aspect of frayed edges and ageing is seen in old clothing, quilts and embroideries which have been used, worn, washed and hung in the sun many times to produce some very interesting and unexpected results. Consider the impressions made by fading, washing and thinning of old quilts and clothing over a period of time giving them such characteristics as seams coming apart, holes, frayed bits and even stains, holes, mending and darning. These effects have become desirable and are now intentionally produced by dyeing, burning, painting and 'distressing' cloth for the background.

A special feature of this book is a project for a concertina stitch-book made from small collages made into 'pages'. The collages are made by sampling the different techniques in your own way or inspired and guided by the photos and diagrams. Another feature is the way that the stitches of each project are translated into clear diagrams showing dimensions and patterns. By drawing, copying or tracing stitches by hand-sketching, new patterns are discovered and a clearer understanding is achieved. Exercises showing how to do this are given in 'learning to see' in Section 2.

## Where to start

I suggest that you browse through the book first to get an overall impression of the instructions and projects, then read

**Section 1**, which lists all the materials and threads needed to do this type of embroidery, how to prepare frames and hoops for stitching, as well as laundering and pressing.

**Section 2** aims to stimulate your creativity with exercises called 'learning to see' and creating a project, from selecting and preparing the fabrics, cutting and tearing them into strips, tacking and stitching the background together, to transferring the design to fabric. It also covers selecting threads for colour, texture and impact and describes the process for creating a project, the elements of perspective, tonal values and the twelve-part colour wheel.

**Section 3** describes ways to create backgrounds by overlapping and layering fabrics, showing many different stitches for securing and decorating edges and merging the background together. Beautiful textiles are created in projects for a stitched and beaded bag, a gift wrap, a colour wash textile and book page.

Aquamarine *wrapped and beaded neckpiece, page 92*

**Section 4** provides instructions for creating beautiful textures and effects with stitches, wrapping, beads, chopped silk, metallic threads, cords, and folded and pleated ribbon and organza.

**Section 5** shows how to make and apply many types of wrapped and beaded cords for embellishment, trimming and an unusual neckpiece.
It also features a continuous cord made with embroidery threads and needle-wrapped while it is attached to the fabric; its many applications are explored in Project 22 'Waves and diamonds' to create a wealth of unique texture for three-dimensional effects.

**Section 6** on bead patterns gives instructions for applying beads in creative ways with stitches, appliqué, ribbons, and cords.

**Section 7** gives instructions for finishing bags, banners and cloth books and for making beaded pendants and fringes, tassels and twisted cords.

**Section 8** provides clear instructions and diagrams for all the stitches used in this book including general stitch hints, soft and hard buttonholed rings and an insertion stitch for joining bags or book pages.
Relax and enjoy the process of creating soft textile collages and embellishing them with stitches, quilting, beads and cords.

*Experience a process of creating where each application allows the surface to evolve*

*from the first layer upwards with a sense of playfulness and thinking outside the square.*

# materials, threads & equipment

This section provides details of equipment, materials, threads, beads and bits, as well as laundering and pressing. It is the starting point to be used in conjunction with all the projects.

# fabrics, threads, cords, beads & bits

The materials and threads I suggest for the various projects are not strictly specific, so that you the embroiderer may use whatever materials and threads you have to hand or choose to purchase. Create or extend a 'stash' of fabrics and threads that you like—whether bought, swapped, recycled or inherited. Add to it as desired. Surround yourself with reflections of your own personal taste and style.

### lining fabric

Indian cotton muslin is a thin, gauzy fabric. Quilter's muslin is too heavy for this technique. Different qualities and thicknesses are available at fabric shops; if the weave is too open, two or more layers may be used together for the lining. The muslin allows ease of stitching and gives a distinctive soft, textured finish to the surface. I use two layers of medium-weight muslin for the first layer/lining.

### fabrics for collage

The silk fabrics dupion and habutai are mostly used. Large pieces are not necessary and scraps and odd-shaped pieces work very well. Silk fabrics are very attractive when the edges are frayed to reveal the two colours woven together to produce the final colour. The frayed warp and weft edges harmonise or contrast with the colour of the woven fabric and suggest ready-made colour schemes. Organza ribbons or organza fabrics by the metre (yard), torn into strips and laid over other fabrics, create subtle variations and depths of colour that work naturally together. Avoid crystal organza as it is reflective.

Extra pattern and texture may be added with scraps of velvet, patterned and embroidered 'after five' and evening fabrics, glitzy fabrics, braids and ribbons.

*Top*: *silks and muslin (white) fabrics;* ***above***: *organza;* ***below left***: *metallic threads & cords;* ***below right***: *ribbons*

### threads for embroidery

Almost any threads may be used for embroidery, merging and embellishments, such as stranded and perle cottons and silks, rayon and silk embroidery threads and twisted silks in different thicknesses as well as knitting and fancy yarns. Metallic threads provide richness and brightness and are available in many varieties and thicknesses, some are suitable for stitching while others need to be couched to the fabric.

A large range of silk ribbons for embroidery, 2 to 4 mm (1/16–3/16 in) wide, is available; these ribbons produce unique stitch textures.

*Different types of threads: stranded cottons, silks and rayons.*

### cords for embellishment and finishing

All types of cords are suitable for embellishment and finishing, among them metallic twisted cords in various thicknesses, rat-tail, Russia braid and more. They are found in craft stores and shops selling gift wrapping, haberdashery–even cake decorating equipment—and other unexpected places as well as on the internet.

### beads

All types of beads are suitable. There are round dress beads in small, medium and large sizes, and bugle beads which are available in many lengths. Larger beads in many shapes and sizes provide very attractive features and textures on designs and trimmings such as the wrapped and beaded cord.

Many accessories and bead trays are available. A useful item is a simple bead tray, which may be made from velvet or felt glued to a paper or plastic plate or the lid of on ice-cream container.

### beading thread and beeswax

Special beading thread, available on small bobbins, is strong and easy to thread through beading needles. Alternatively use sewing cotton size 50 drawn through beeswax for strengthening after threading it through the needle. Use colours of thread to match or contrast with the beads.

*Cutting mat, rotary cutter and plastic ruler for cutting out fabrics, fabric/craft glue, couronne (ring) stick, quick unpick, tracing paper (kitchen greaseproof), rulers, plastic or metal rings, paper and fabric scissors, masking tape, tape measure.*

### beading needles

Beading needles or size 10 embroidery needles are fine enough to pull the thread through small beads. When using machine sewing cotton, thread the needle first and pull it once or twice through the beeswax before using.

### embroidery frame

A roller frame as shown in the photo is recommended.

### embroidery hoop

A comfortable hoop size for average hands is 15–18 cm (6–7 in).

### light

It is important for any type of embroidery that good lighting is used, either daylight or an adjustable lamp focused on the work. (If you find you cannot work in good light without developing eyestrain, a check-up with the optometrist is indicated.)

### quick unpick

This is a handy dressmaker's tool for quickly unpicking stitches.

### needles

*Embroidery needles* (also called 'crewel needles') come in many sizes and are

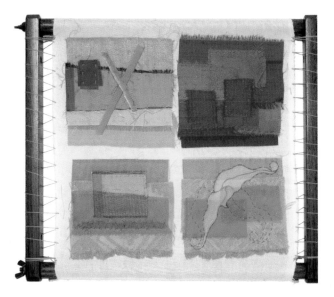

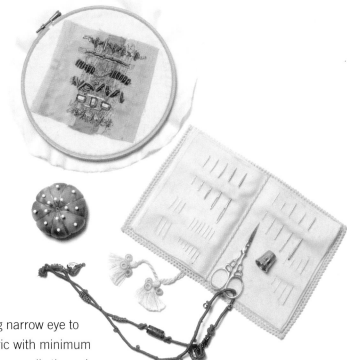

*Roller frame, embroidery hoop, pins, needles, embroidery scissors, thimble.*

suitable for surface stitches. They have sharp points and a long narrow eye to carry the thread and facilitate ease of passage through the fabric with minimum irritation of the thread. Use a size which allows the thread to pass easily through the eye, without being too loose in the eye, and makes a hole large enough for the thread to pass through without damaging it. Generally sizes 1 to 9 (the smallest number referring to the largest size) provide a good range. Specialty shops can provide larger needles for very thick threads and yarns.

• **Milliners/straw needles**, which are long and smooth, are ideal for bullion stitch.
• **Tapestry needles** have a large eye and a blunt point that will not split the threads of the fabric, making them ideal for wrapping and whipping over stitches. They are available in sizes 16 to 26, the smallest number referring to the largest size.
• **Chenille needles** are available in the same shapes and sizes as tapestry needles; the difference is that they have a sharp point. They are also used to take couched metal threads to the back of the work.
• **Beading needles**: refer to beads above.

Note that needle sizes may vary between brands.

## other equipment

Rulers: metal or plastic

Scissors: for fabric, embroidery and paper

Tape measure

Pins

Thimble

Tracing paper: stationery products and kitchen greaseproof are suitable for tracing designs and transferring them to fabric

Couronne (ring) stick: for embroidered 'soft' buttonholed rings

Rings, plastic or metal: for embroidered 'hard' buttonholed rings

masking tape

# mounting fabric in frames and hoops

Different effects are achieved depending on whether the fabric is held taut in a frame or hoop or held in the hand. There may be a personal preference involved because of familiarity or ease of stitching. However, different effects result from each method.

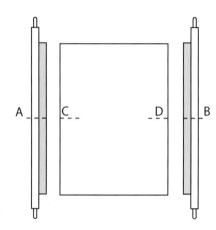

*Mounting fabric to a frame: the side-bars*

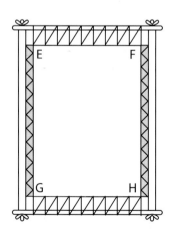

*Mounting fabric to a frame: the cross-bars*

- Stitching with the fabric held taut in a frame results in a smoother embroidered surface. Stitching on fabric held in a hoop can often result in undulations on the surface of the fabric.
- Stitching on fabric in the hand and pulling stitches tighter results in more prominent waves and undulations.

## frame

A good size to handle is a frame with 30.5 cm (12 in) rollers and cross-bars of approximately 33 cm (13 in). Larger works are mounted in larger frames or made in smaller sections for assembly later. The tension of the rollers is controlled by washers and butterfly nuts.

It is recommended that the first layer/lining be attached and laced to the frame before adding subsequent layers of fabric and stitching. Follow these steps to mount fabric to a frame:

1 Remove the washers and nuts and separate the two rollers.
2 Mark the rollers in the centre at A and B with pen or pencil.
3 Cut out one or more layers of muslin for the lining, place the layers on top of one another and stitch them together around the edges with either zigzag or over-locking.
4 Fold the fabric in half and mark with pins the centres on two opposite sides of the lining which are to be attached to the roller tape, C and D.
5 Pin the fabric to the roller tape matching the centre marks, A and C, D and B.
6 Stitch the lining to the roller tape with a wide, long machine zigzag stitch (width 4, length 2). After the work is completed this stitching is removed with a quick unpick.
7 Attach the cross-bars and screw them in place.
8 Using 4-ply non-stretch knitting/crochet cotton or other thread equal in thickness to perle 5 (not sewing cotton or fine thread) and a large needle, lace the fabric to the two bars of the frame, between E and F, and G and H. Don't cut the thread off the ball until the lacing is complete, so that one continuous length of yarn is used on each side.
9 Tighten the tension of the lacing stitches, making sure that the fabric is straight and parallel to the bars before tying off the lacing thread. Tighten the rollers, and adjust them as needed while stitching.

### hoop

Bind the inner ring with bias binding or cotton tape before using the hoop to ensure that your work will be held firmly in place.

1 Cut one or more squares of muslin lining 10 cm (4 in) larger than the hoop.
2 Cut the corners off to make a circle 5 cm larger than the hoop.
3 Place the lining pieces on a flat surface and tack them together before placing them in a hoop.

# laundering and pressing

Unexpected results may occur when laundering a mixture of materials, threads, metallic threads and beads. The safest, gentle washing procedure is as follows:

*Silk fabrics are available in a wide range of rich, vibrant colours.*

- Hand-wash each piece gently and separately in warm to cool water, using pure or mild soap. Avoid using any detergent with a blueing or bleaching agent.
- During the washing, if the water becomes coloured, continue to wash with cold water and rinse thoroughly several times while holding the embroidery right side downwards, allowing the rinsing water to flow through from the back.
- Roll in a thick towel to remove excess moisture.
- Dry flat on a towel in the shade.

A spray of a fine mist of water sprayed onto silk fabric facilitates the removal of creases and folds.

After the work is complete, pressing with an iron may not be necessary if a natural, textured effect is chosen. The safest method is to use a fine cotton fabric or several layers of muslin as a pressing cloth between the iron and the article, particularly when metallic threads are used.

For textured articles place them face down onto a clean, folded bath towel and press on the back. The bath towel absorbs the texture.

# 2

# learning to see

Learning to see is part of developing creativity. The visual images we make give an insight and understanding into how we work. They reveal our own unique sense of style and with repetition allow it to flower and grow.

# learning to see

Two exercises for expanding our ability to see are outlined in this section: tracing and drawing patterns, and tracing and drawing stitches.

Many of us think we can't draw but most of us are able to write, doodle and scribble. And there are rulers for straight lines, graph paper and templates for circles and geometric patterns, tracing paper, photocopying machines and computer programs to help and speed the process. Visual resources such as a visual diary, pencils, pens and paint are some of the tools to work with. (A *visual diary* is a record of what you see, what attracts you and what you favour.) Add a sense of play and remember or imagine what it was, or would have been, like when you 'just did it' in kindergarten. Approach these exercises with a sense of fun, just do them to the best of your ability and enjoy.

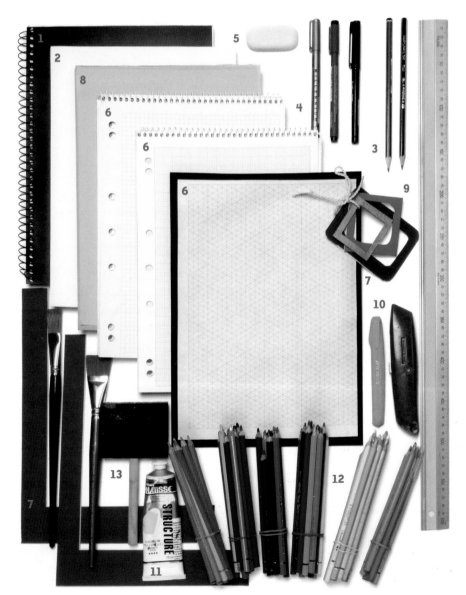

### materials and equipment for learning to see

*1 Visual diary A4 size*
*2 printing paper A4 size*
*3 pencils HB*
*4 pens, drawing sizes 0.04 to 0.08*
*5 eraser*
*6 graph paper, different sizes, including 'isometric graph paper' which is ideal for triangles and hexagons*
*7 windows: square, rectangle, circle, two "L's", etc. (make your own from thick card, any size)*
*8 tracing paper, (book form)*
*9 heavy metal ruler*
*10 cutting knife, craft or Stanley*
*11 watercolour or acrylic paint for colour-washing pages: yellow ochre is a good general background colour to start with*
*12 coloured or water-soluble coloured pencils*
*13 sponges and/or paint brushes*

# learning to see

*Colour-washed paper with patterns and butterfly by the author*

Remember also that practice and repetition improve understanding, skill and speed. Although the patterns may never actually be used the exercises, like practising the piano, increase perception and the ability to discern pattern, lines and shapes.

Not shown in the photograph are resources for images, which may be photos, pictures from books and magazines such as gardens, landscapes, jewellery, architecture and so on, or a light box or glass-topped table with lamp underneath or a glass door or window which make tracing so much easier.

## colour wash paper

Dilute a little paint with water in a dish or jar and apply it to the paper with sponges or brushes. You can quickly begin your visual diary by painting a number of pages, separating them with paper towels and drying them in the sun or with a hair dryer.

The colour may be built up by lightly shading the wash with coloured or water-soluble coloured pencils. You can also shade pages with coloured pencils without the wash.

## tracing and drawing patterns

Select an image by placing a 'window' over it.

- Photocopy it the same size, reduce or enlarge it.
- Trace or draw the patterns from the photocopy onto plain or colour-wash pages in the visual diary.
- Repeat this exercise in as many ways as you wish.

## tracing and drawing stitches

The purpose of this exercise is not only to get the feel of the mark and rhythm of stitches and achieve a closer understanding of how they are made but to explore, by a method that is quicker than actually stitching, the scale, repetitive patterns, extensions, distortions and anything else one can think of or discover in the process.

- Divide a page of graph, printing or visual diary into squares or other divisions
- Choose stitches from this or other books and trace or draw them freehand onto one of the sections. Change the scale, make repetitive patterns, extend, overlap and/or distort them.
- Repeat this exercise in as many ways as you wish.

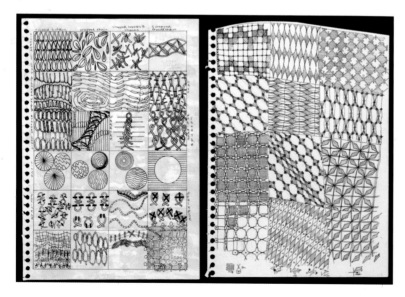

**Left:** *stitch drawing and doodling* **Right:** *Stitch patterns drawn onto an irregular grid by the author from an early 20th century runner in the collection of The Embroiderers' Guild NSW Inc., Sydney, Australia*

# creating a project

Creating embroidery is a process, a series of decisions made in accordance with the availability and selection of threads, fabrics, beads and stitches that we have or need to buy.

The decision making is actually a process of elimination. Many embroiderers say 'but I don't know what I want', and 'I'm not creative'. We may not know what we want but we certainly know what we don't want—and this is the place to start.

The process of creating a project is divided into sections—creating the background, threads for merging backgrounds, threads for embroidery, threads for colour texture and impact, choosing colours and contrasting elements that create perspective and interest, and transferring the design to the fabric.

## creating the background
*It is recommended that this section be used in conjunction with instructions for all projects.*

**step 1** Gather together the requirements for the background.
- Fabrics—silk dupion, silk habutai, organza and any other rich, patterned or glitzy fabrics
- Muslin lining, two or more layers depending on the weight of the muslin and your preference (I most often use two pieces)
- Pins, sewing cottons to match fabric
- Needles: embroidery size 5 and 7 or larger as needed
- Fabric and paper scissors
- Tracing paper

**step 2** Select fabrics
- Place all the fabrics to be considered onto a table.
- One by one, pick up a fabric and ask yourself the questions 'Yes?', 'No?', 'Maybe?', and allocate each fabric to a bundle called 'yes', 'no' and 'maybe'.
- After this, put away the 'no' bundle.
- Go through all the fabrics in the 'maybe' bundle and repeat the questions again and again until only 'yes' fabrics remain.
- Sort the 'yes' fabrics into groups by colour or tone (light, medium, dark)

**step 3** Tear and cut strips of fabric
Add 2 cm (¾ in) to the width of each strip to allow for overlapping of 1 cm (⅜ in) on each side.
- Tear silk along the grain after first cutting in at the edge for 2 cm (¾ in). Remove threads from the torn edges to create fringing.
- Cut strips of fabrics that cannot be torn with sharp scissors, and other fabrics for a different effect from tearing.

*Strips of cut and torn silk and organza and ribbon*

# creating a project

*'Yellow cross': tacking stitches and selvedge edges applied as a cross*

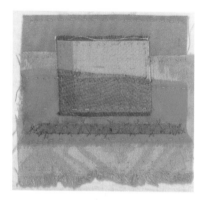

*'Orange, blue and violet ribbon': run-stitched edges of collage*

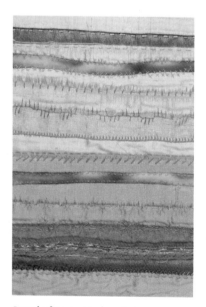

*Detail of Project 1 showing a background of cut and torn strips of silk and organza, and ribbon*

- Incorporate the selvedge edge or cut it off and store it for later application on a collage to achieve a distinctive effect. The photo captioned 'Yellow cross' shows selvedge edges applied as a cross.
- Vary the width of the strips for interest, for example 2, 3, 4.5, 5, 6 and 7.5 cm (¾, 1 ³⁄₁₆, 1 ¾, 2, 2 ⅜, and 3 in). Press the strips before applying to the muslin lining.

### step 4  First layer (lining)
Cut muslin lining and mount in a frame or hoop. Overlock or zigzag stitch the edges and mount muslin into a frame before applying the fabric collage, or apply the fabric collage to muslin before placing in the hoop.

### step 5  Second layer (fabric collage)
Lay the cut or torn strips of silk or other rich fabrics of varying widths on top of the first layer (lining). Stagger edges for an integrated look and avoid strong diagonal lines. There are, of course, exceptions to any rule, as can be seen in the photo 'Yellow cross', where a diagonal cross is applied.

### step 6  Third layer (added extras)
Add cut or torn strips of organza and/or ribbons or ribbon-like yarns vertically and/or horizontally (as seen in the detail of Project 1) across the middle or over the edges of silk strips to create more variations of colours and texture. Again stagger the edges for an integrated look and avoid strong diagonal lines. Note how the frayed edge of the organza in front of the green and yellow creates a third colour blend in 'Orange, blue and violet ribbon'. The detail of Project 1 includes all the elements (except staggered edges) in one background. Staggered edges appear in Project 14 'Ancient Eyes', Project 16 'Butterfly', Project 22 'Waves and Diamonds', and most book pages.

### step 7  Pin and tack
When you are happy with the result, pin all the elements together and tack with sewing cotton or one strand of cotton in a closely matching colour. Make the tacking stitches 3 mm (⅛ in) long on the front and 2.5 cm (1 in) at the back to minimise their impact on the colour scheme and avoid possibly affecting decisions regarding colour choices. Remove them as the work progresses. If the tacking stitches blend well they may not need to be removed. 'Yellow cross' shows a collage tacked in place.

### merging stitches
Collaged backgrounds may be stitched with a minimum of stitches to hold them together or lots of stitches for a decorative surface.
The edges of strips of overlapping fabrics may be stitched as in Project 1 'Green and blue collage', or you can use running stitches 3 mm (⅛ in) from the edge

of all the shapes in matching colours as shown in the photos 'Orange, blue and violet ribbon' and 'Red patches'.

Refer to the projects in Section 3 Backgrounds for other methods of merging and decorating the background.

### threads for merging backgrounds

One or more colours may be used to merge the background. One strand of cotton or silk in a colour to match the fabric provides the most subdued effect. Two or more strands together in the needle create more texture and are therefore more prominent.

When only one colour of thread is used over the background, interesting colour contrasts can be made as the stitches meander across different coloured fabrics, as in Project 22 'Waves and Diamonds'.

*'Red patches': overlapped edges with running stitch, the same form of background collage used in Project 6 'Butterflies out of a box'*

# threads for colour, texture and impact

Almost any threads may be used for embroidery, merging and embellishments, including stranded cotton, rayon and silk embroidery threads, perle cotton, and the many fancy yarns which are available in single, space-dyed and variegated colours.

Metallic threads provide richness and brightness and are available in many varieties and thickness; some are suitable for stitching while others need to be couched onto the fabric.

A large range of silk ribbons for embroidery, 4–7 mm ($\frac{5}{16}$–¼ in) wide, is available and produces unique textures.

Some knitting yarns also provide very attractive and suitable threads for embroidery.

### effie's magic and zinger colours

The colours of rich silk are enhanced with a palette of 'magic' colours which are reflected in the DMC embroidery thread range and have been specially selected for purity to match the vibrancy of the colours of silk. They are yellow 728, 729, 3820 and 783, electric blue 995, 3843, 3844, 3845, violet 552, 333 and 3746, orange 920 and 720, yellow green 581 and 733, turquoise 597, magenta red 601, 917 and 718, terracotta 356, ruby 321, aquamarine 958 and 3849. Stranded threads in these colours work very well for merging and blending backgrounds.

Two 'zingers' I particularly like using, although they can seem rather shocking on their own, are DMC 995 electric blue and DMC 718 hot pink.

# choosing colours

For a better understanding of colour proportions and relationships, when you are selecting threads to match fabrics, place only one length of thread, not a whole skein or ball, across the fabric.

In general, choose colours because you like them. Colour schemes may be inspired simply by choosing your favourite colours, choosing monochromatic or tonal variations of one colour, harmonious or contrasting colours, colours in nature and the seasons.

Jewel colours such as ruby, turquoise, amethyst, amber, topaz and emerald, whether used singly or together, ideally match the vibrant and striking colours of pure silk.

Without restricting your choices, a limited range of colours for the background such as monochromatic (tonal values of one colour) or harmonious (values of two or three adjoining colours on the colour wheel) are beautiful combinations. To create depth and perspective to a colour scheme be aware of the tonal values of one colour. Tonal values of light through to dark shades create perspective through the light/dark contrast whereby lighter colours 'come forward' and are more prominent than darker shades. Three or more tonal variations of the one colour create greater depth.

- Harmonious colours—two or three harmonious colours incorporating tonal values of each of the three colours create more contrast than monochromatic.
- Complementary colours–colours opposite each other on the colour wheel create the strongest contrasts of colour when used together.

*Cocoons soaking for unwinding silk, silk weaving factory, China*

### ready-made colour schemes

The warp and weft of silk fabrics are often woven with different colours so that in one piece of fabric there are three colours—the warp, the weft and the colour resulting from the mix. By fraying the edges the colours of both warp and weft are revealed, suggesting a harmonious or complementary colour scheme. Other colour schemes may be inspired by flowers, landscapes or seascapes, the seasons or by richly woven fabrics.

### contrasting elements create perspective and interest

This section provides a general understanding of elements of perspective, but is a guide only as there are always exceptions.

Perspective is heightened when the illusion of areas receding or coming forward is created by contrasting light with dark tonal values, warm with cool colours, shiny with matt surfaces, bright with dull colours, large with small scales of shapes and stitches, thick with thin and/or rough with smooth threads.

### thick/thin

*Bowlfuls of silk 'cocoons'*

One strand of cotton or silk is thick enough to make an impact. For a stronger effect use two or more strands, perle cottons, silk or rayon, or different threads combined together. Shiny yarns such as rayon and silk are reflective and therefore more noticeable than a matt finish.

## pattern/plain

More pattern is created and the effect more noticeable when one or two strands of cotton, or silk in contrasting colours (pattern) to the fabric, are used compared with a matching colour (plain). More pattern is created with the use of variegated or space-dyed threads. More texture and pattern are created with the use of thicker and uneven threads, still more when they are variegated or space-dyed.

## shiny/matt

Shiny threads such as silk and rayon contrasted with matt thread such as stranded cotton and perle stand out more as they reflect light and thus appear brighter.

## light/dark

Lighter values stand out more when used with darker colours—backgrounds recede when lighter colours are applied. The contrast is stronger when the tonal values are further apart on the tonal scale of white through to black. Understanding the tonal value of a colour, that is, the level of dark and light as demonstrated in the tonal value scale, is a valuable tool for achieving balance. When in doubt, photograph the colours in black and white.

## tonal value scale

| | |
|---|---|
| | white |
| | high light — very light |
| | LIGHT |
| | low light — medium light |
| | middle grey — medium |
| | high dark — medium dark |
| | DARK |
| | low dark — very dark |
| | black |

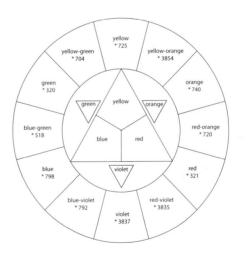

### stitched twelve-part colour wheel

*Clockwise from the top: yellow, yellow-orange, orange, orange-red, red, red-violet, violet, blue-violet, blue, blue-green, green, yellow-green*

### pattern for twelve-part colour wheel

*The threads used are DMC stranded cotton.
Starting at the top, clockwise: 725 yellow, 3854 yellow-orange, 740 orange, 720 red-orange, 321 red, 3835 red-violet, 3837 violet, 792 blue-violet, 798 blue, 518 blue-green, 320 green, 704 yellow-green.*

enlarge
by 200%
diameter
approx
12cm
(4 ¾ in)

## choosing colours

suggested exercise

*Transfer the outline of the colour wheel onto white linen fabric and stitch the colour wheel. The colour wheel shown is stitched as follows:*

***Primary colours**, the large triangles and corresponding panels (yellow at 12 o'clock), red (4 o'clock) and blue (8 o'clock): double detached chain stitches (two stitches worked one around the other) using 6 strands and gaps filled with French knots.*

***Secondary colours**, the small triangles and corresponding panels: French knots with 3, 6 and 9 strands in the needle.*

***Tertiary colours**, between primary and secondary colours: wavy lines of chain stitch.*

### warm/cool

Warmer colours (red, red-violet, orange and orange-red) are more prominent relative to cooler colours (blue, blue-violet and green). Violet is the darkest colour on the colour wheel, and varies from warm red-violet to cool blue-violet. Its opposite, yellow, is the lightest colour on the colour wheel.
If a design appears too subdued it may need a touch of warmth or brightness.

### brightness

Shades of yellow are the lightest and brightest colours and need to be used with discretion on backgrounds, although subdued yellows such as mustard, topaz and yellow ochre are often suitable. A wide range of tonal values and shades of yellow are available because it is the lightest colour in the colour wheel. The range is extended because of earthy yellow ochre and widened when it is mixed with green (for a cooler effect) or red (for a warmer effect). If a design appears to be too subdued it may need a touch of warm yellow or other warm colours.

# transferring design to fabric

*An early stage in a version of Project 23 'Sinuous shapes': transferring the design to fabric*

1 Photocopy or trace the design onto tracing paper, and cut, following the outline all around the design.
2 Pin the tracing paper onto the fabric and make small running stitches around the shapes with a contrasting colour that is easy to see.
3 Cut away sections of the paper as you complete the stitching, and outline the remaining shapes until the design is completely transferred.
4 The stitches are pulled out as the embroidery progresses.

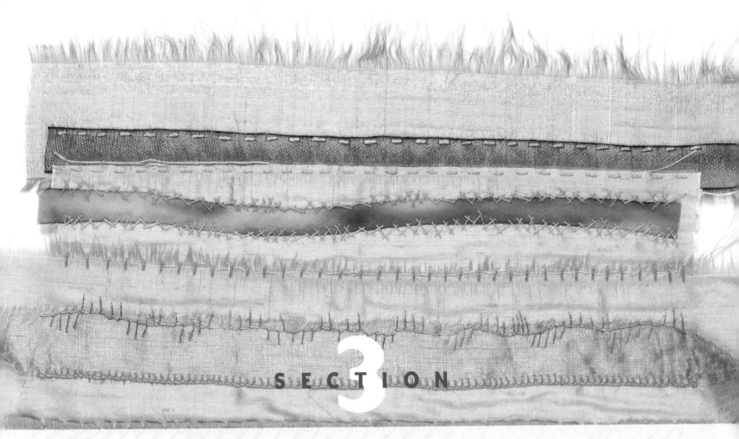

# backgrounds

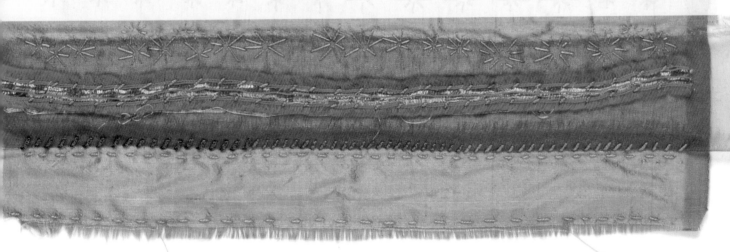

This section provides instructions on how to create backgrounds for embroidery.
As it is the first project recommended as a starting point the instructions
are specific to 'making a background of overlapped and layered fabrics'.
Even though they are similar to those in Section 2
'Creating a project' it is recommended that both instructions
be used in conjunction with this and all projects.

# green & blue 1 collage with stitched edges

The aim of this project is to create a collage of overlapped and layered fabric as a background for embroidery and a vocabulary of stitches to secure, decorate and enhance raw, frayed, turned and selvedge edges.

## finished size of collage
## 25 x 24 cm (9 ⅞ x 9 ½ in)

### materials

■ Indian muslin for lining 30 x 20 cm (11 ¾ x 7 ⅞ in); use 1, 2 or more layers depending on the weight of the muslin and your preference; zigzag stitch or overlock the edges of the layers together before attaching to a frame (first layer/lining)

■ Silk dupion and/or other rich fabrics: various widths of strips 2.5 to 7.5 cm (1 to 3 in) (instructions below for preparing strips of fabric)

■ Silk or other ribbons or yarns

■ Organza, transparent or semi transparent: strips of torn organza or purchased organza ribbons

■ Embroidery threads and yarns such as stranded cotton, perle 8 or 12, stranded or perle silk and rayon in colours to match or contrast the fabrics

■ Sewing cotton or 1 strand embroidery cotton for tacking

■ Embroidery frame 30.5 cm (12 in) or Embroidery hoop 15–18 cm (6–7 in)

■ Pins

■ Needles: embroidery, assorted sizes 1 to 9 or larger as needed

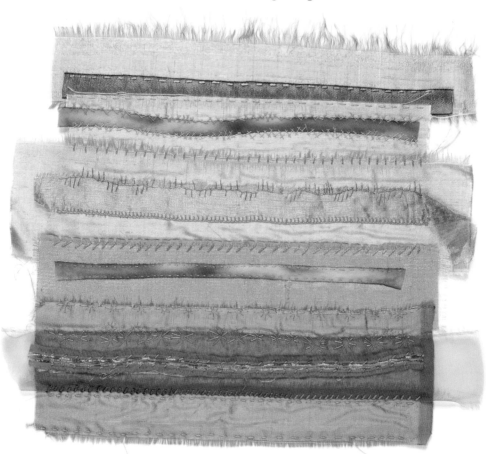

## making a background of overlapped and layered fabrics

Make the collage before stitching in the hoop, OR on the framed lining.

### preparing strips of fabric

Allow 2 cm (¾ in) extra on the width of each strip for overlapping of 1 cm (⅜ in) on each side.

• **Tearing strips** Attractive edges are made by tearing silk dupion along the grain after first cutting the edge for 6–12 mm (½ or 1 in). Remove fabric threads from the edges to create fringing.

• **Cutting strips** With sharp scissors cut strips of fabrics that cannot be torn, or for a different effect from tearing.

### lining and layering the background

• **First layer/lining** Lay one or two layers of cotton muslin on a flat surface (for hoop) or mount it in a frame.

• **Second layer (layering)** Lay cut or torn strips of silk or other rich fabrics of varying widths on top of the first layer (lining) overlapping the edges 1 cm (⅜ in). Refer to the diagram with the following project, showing the width of the strips. Vary the width of the strips for interest, between 2–7.5 cm (¾–3 in) wide, for example 2, 3, 4.5, 5, 6 and 7.5 cm (¾, 1 ³⁄₁₆, 1 ¾, 2, 2 ⅜, and 3 in). Press the strips before applying to the lining.

• **Third layer (added layers)** of cut or torn strips of organza and/or ribbons or ribbon-like yarns may be placed across middle or over the edges of silk strips to create more variations of colours and texture,

When you are happy with the result, pin and tack them all together with sewing cotton or 1 strand cotton in a closely matching colour. Make the tacking stitches 3 mm (⅛ in) long on the front and 2.5cm (1 in) at the back to minimise their impact on the colour scheme. If they blend well there is no need to remove them as the work progresses.

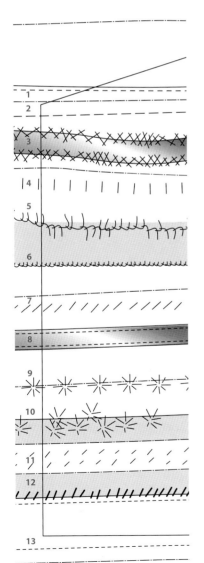

*A harmonious colour scheme of green and blue is made from different widths of raw, frayed, turned and selvedge edges of silk fabrics layered with overlapped edges, added ribbons and organza, and edges secured and decorated with stitches as follows:*

1   *Running stitch with 1 strand silk equal to perle 8*

2   *Running stitch with 1 strand cotton*

3   *Herringbone stitch on both sides of a silk ribbon with 1 strand cotton*

4   *Straight stitch, vertical with rayon perle equal to perle 8*

5   *Blanket stitch, up and down, with 1 strand space-dyed silk*

6   *Blanket stitch with rayon perle equal to perle 8*

7   *Straight stitch, diagonal with silk equal to perle 5*

8   *Running stitches with 1 strand cotton on edges of silk ribbon*

9   *Straight stitch eyelets with 1 strand cotton*

10  *Straight stitch eyelets with 1 strand cotton, in random sizes and spaces*

11  *Straight stitch, diagonal, 2 rows on a ribbon yarn with rayon perle equal to perle 8*

12  *Straight stitch, diagonal over a folded edge of organza (worked with edge held away), the left-hand section with rayon cord equal to perle 3, the middle section with cotton perle 8 and the right-hand section with 3 strands cotton*

13  *Running stitch with rayon perle equal to perle 8*

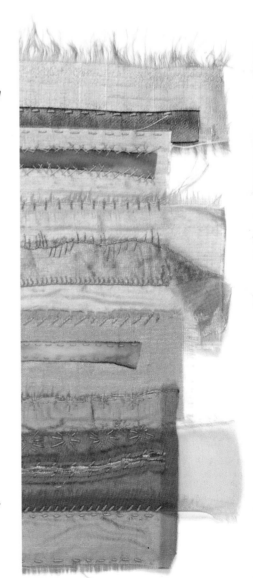

# green & blue 1

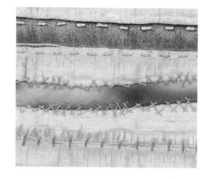

## stitches for edges

Decorate the edges using the stitches as described in the stitch illustration. Different patterns are made by each stitch. Running stitch is the most subtle, followed by herringbone stitch which is more textured, while buttonhole stitch is even more textured and noticeable. The characteristics and impact of each stitch are clearly seen on the diagram. Horizontal stitches are more restful, vertical are neutral, diagonal and eyelets create more movement and herringbone, up and down blanket and random eyelets give more texture.

# green & blue 2 stitched & beaded bag

This project shows how to embellish a collaged and stitched background with beads and make it into a bag with a wrapped and beaded cord.

## pattern for green & blue bag

 silk ribbon
(Rows 3 and 8)

organza (Rows 6 and 10-12 and row 11, with ribbon applied to top of organza)

edges of fabric, including fraying

enlarge or reduce diagram to suit

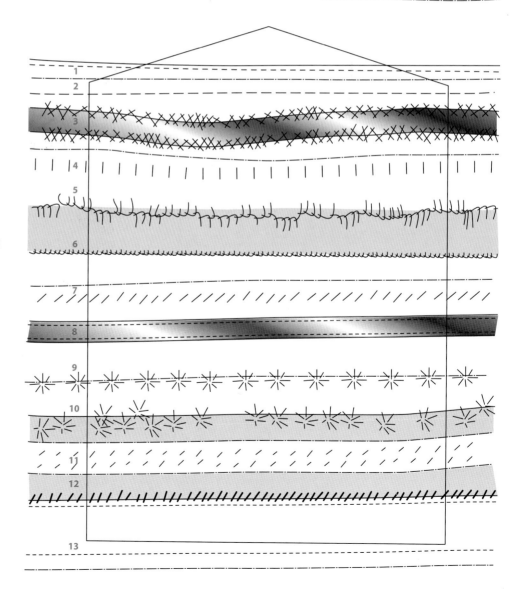

The background collage of this bag is shown on the diagram for project 1 as it is the same. Reduce or enlarge the pattern to suit your purpose and tack the outline of the bag onto the background.

Embellish the background with bead patterns.
See Section 6, Stitch and bead patterns.

Make up the bag following directions in Section 7, Finishing and making up.

Attach a bought cord or make a wrapped and beaded cord. See Section 5, Cords for embellishment and trimming. The wrapped and beaded cords in the photo consist of two cords 90 cm (35 ½ in) long, one made in DMC 6 stranded cotton colour 597, the other in colour 733. The core and wrapping are made from 8 lengths of 6-stranded cotton and a string of blue and green beads. Trim the threads at each end of the cords to make a tassel and tie an overhand knot at each end. The two cords are folded in half and looped together at the midway point at the top of the bag and attached double to the sides of the bag with slip stitch in 1 strand of the same colour.

# blue & orange

running stitch patterns for merging & blending backgrounds

## materials

■ Indian muslin for the first layer (lining), 36 x 30 cm (14 1/8 x 11 ¾ in): 1, 2 or more layers depending on the weight of the muslin and your preference; zigzag stitch or overlock the edges of all layers together before attaching to the frame (first layer/ lining)

■ Silk dupion or other suitable fabric 35 x 26 cm (13 ¾ x 10 ¼ in) for the background (second layer)

■ 12 squares silk dupion or other suitable fabric, each 5.5 cm (2 ⅛ in) square, lightly frayed edges (third layer)

■ Silk, organza and/or ribbons or flat yarns (fourth layer)

■ Embroidery threads: stranded cotton or silk, perle 8

■ Sewing cotton or one strand cotton embroidery cotton for tacking

■ Beads

■ Beading needle

■ Beading thread (or size 50 sewing cotton pulled through beeswax)

■ Embroidery frame, 30.5 cm (12 in)

■ Pins

■ Needles; embroidery, assorted sizes 3 to 9 or larger as needed

Running stitch is a versatile basic stitch and many patterns and textures can be made by:

• Changing the way the fabric is held, in a frame, a hoop or in the hand

• Varying the tension at which the stitch is pulled or tightened

• Varying the evenness or lengths of stitches

• Varying the spaces between the stitches

• Varying the thickness of thread: one strand of embroidery cotton in a size 7 embroidery needle gives a very subtle background, while 2 strands of cotton, perle or rayon threads together in a larger embroidery needle make a much stronger impact.

Different effects can be achieved by:
• Stitching with the fabric held taut in a frame or hoop, which results in a smooth surface of stitch pattern as shown in the photo for this project
• Stitching while holding the fabric in the hand produces undulations in the fabric created by the patterns of the stitch, as shown here in the detail from 'Spirals, shells and beads' (a project not included in this book).

• Stitching while holding the fabric in the hand and pulling stitches tighter creates more prominent waves and undulations in the patterns of the stitch, as shown in here in the detail of a long yellow strip with running stitch.

*Detail from 'Spirals, shells and beads': running stitch, medium tension*

The background for this project consists of four layers:
• The first layer (lining) is of one or more pieces of muslin, 36 x 30 cm (14 1/8 x 11 ¾ in)
• The second layer is the background fabric, a rectangle of silk, 35 x 26 cm (13 ¾ x 10 ¼ in)
• The third layer is twelve squares of silk fabric, each 5.5 cm (2 1/8 in) square, in colours to match or contrast with the background, edges lightly frayed, spaced 6 mm (1/2 in) apart.
• The fourth layer is small pieces of fabric on top of each square.

Each square is stitched with different patterns and sizes of running stitch. The impact made by the colour and thickness of threads illustrates the different effects achieved by using threads which are thick or thin, light or dark, warm or cool. The colour scheme in this project is a complementary contrast of blue and orange with the addition of scraps of light yellow fabrics in rows 1, 3 and 4 which pick up and reflect the colour of the warp or weft of the fringed fabric squares applied in the third layer.

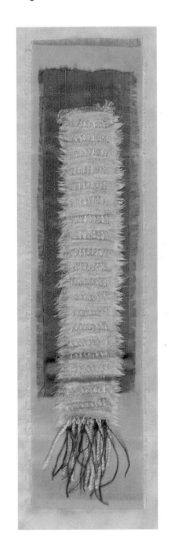

## preparing the background
**First layer** Mount the muslin onto a frame, refer to page 16.

**Second layer** Lay silk 35 x 26 (13 ¾ x 10 ¼ in) on top.

**Third layer** Pin the 12 squares onto the background fabric in four rows of three, approximately 6 mm (¼ in) apart.
Tack these three layers together.

**Fourth layer** Pin scraps of silk and/or organza onto each square. They are only pinned on at this stage as their position may alter as stitching progresses.

## running stitch patterns for merging and blending backgrounds

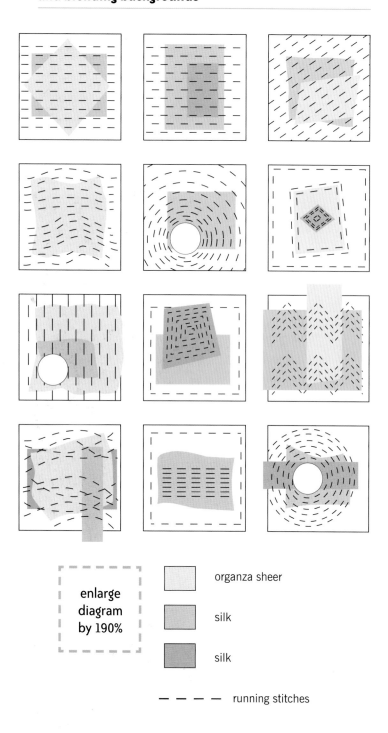

enlarge diagram by 190%

organza sheer

silk

silk

– – – – running stitches

### running stitch patterns

Work running stitches guided by the diagram and photograph of the finished project.

#### row 1

*Left*: even stitches, horizontal parallel rows, 1 strand blue cotton

*Centre*: uneven stitches, brick pattern, horizontal parallel rows, 1 strand orange cotton

*Right*: even stitches, parallel wavy rows, 1strand mid-blue cotton; note how the darker coloured stitching diminishes and subdues the overall impact of the fabrics.

#### row 2

*Left*: wavy lines not parallel, 1 strand orange cotton and blue rayon perle equal to perle 8

*Centre*: a round, flat, shell bead is first applied and concentric circles of running stitch made around it with blue rayon perle equal to perle 8

*Right*: stitches within and outlining applied shapes of fabrics, 1 strand orange and blue cotton

#### row 3

*Left*: vertical parallel rows of long, uneven stitches, 1 strand mid-blue cotton with a round, flat, shell bead applied on top

*Centre*: 'Greek key' spiral pattern with blue rayon perle equal to perle 8

*Right*: zigzag pattern worked with blue rayon perle equal to perle 8 (top) and 1 strand blue cotton (below).

#### row 4

*Left*: wavy, overlapping lines worked with 3 strands blue/green cotton

*Centre*: horizontal parallel rows within an applied shape which highlights the stitches, 1 strand orange cotton

*Right*: a round, flat, shell bead is first applied and a spiralling line of stitches is worked around it in 1 strand blue cotton.

# gift wrap

## running stitch on patterned fabric and running stitch with tension

A square of beautiful hand-made embroidery has many uses—as a gift wrap, bag, cushion front and for a table or chair back. This project celebrates the freedom and joy of stitching in the hand allowing the surface to evolve with moment by moment decision making as it grows.

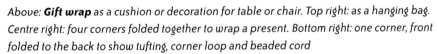

*Above:* **Gift wrap** *as a cushion or decoration for table or chair. Top right: as a hanging bag. Centre right: four corners folded together to wrap a present. Bottom right: one corner, front folded to the back to show tufting, corner loop and beaded cord*

A framework of measurements, and suggestions for stitches, are provided to give impetus for your creative style to emerge. It is an exercise in starting from the first layer and working upwards rather than from a finished result. Techniques to be explored are creating a collage of plain and patterned fabrics and stitching with variations of running stitch using different weights of thread, stitches of various lengths and tension and beading.

The diagram shows the random shapes of the fabrics that have been collaged and the application of sequins in straight lines (A) to balance the uneven fabric

## finished size of collage approx 34 cm (13 ¼ in) square

### materials
Create your own palette of colours.

■ Indian muslin, 44 cm (17 ¼ in) square: 1, 2 or more layers depending on the weight of the muslin and your preference; zigzag stitch or overlock the edges together before attaching to a frame (first layer/lining)

■ Silk dupion, organza and other fabrics for collage

■ Backing fabric for making up and finishing: 2 pieces silk dupion 40 cm (15 ¾ in) square, one for attaching the collage to make the front of the article; the other for the back (these measurements include 3 cm (1 ³/₁₆ in) seam allowance all round)

■ Extra silk dupion or bought cord to make 4 loops for the corners

■ Embroidery threads equal to perle 8 and/or 12 and stranded cottons and/or silk

■ Beads, medium, 4 mm (³/₁₆ in) in diameter with large hole for cord and tufting

■ Sequins, 3 mm (⅛ in) in diameter

■ Beading needle

■ Beading thread (or size 50 sewing cotton pulled through beeswax)

■ Sewing cotton or 1 strand cotton embroidery cotton for tacking

■ Pins

■ Needles: embroidery sizes 1–7 or larger as needed

■ 1.6 m (63 in) beaded and wrapped cord or other cord for threading through corner loops

shapes and stitch patterns. This design may be used as a guide or starting point. Take time to play around with different arrangements of shapes, adding and subtracting here and there until you are satisfied.

Bits and pieces of fabric may be added as the work progresses, more stitches cover the surface and the embroidery evolves and changes direction as mood and intuition direct. Some of the edges are stitched with straight stitches (B). Applied organza strips, some with edges rolled and stitched (C), create subtle colour variations and contrasts of texture.

Tightening thread tension when making running stitches creates undulating ridges, hills and valleys in the fabric. Two different results of fabric manipulation are made by applying tension. When working running stitch in horizontal rows with tight tension the stitches push the fabric in the spaces between the stitches upwards to create hills and ridges (D). By working vertical rows of spaced straight (satin) stitches with tight tension the stitches push the fabric in the spaces between the rows downwards creating valleys (E). These satin stitches are worked in vertical rows from the top down and must be finished off at the end of each vertical row to hold the tension.

Squares of running stitches are worked around motifs on patterned fabric (F) and repeated elsewhere (G).

### method
Collage the fabrics, overlapping edges 1 cm (⅜ in) to finished size of collage 34 cm (13 ¼ in) (second layer), onto muslin (first layer/lining), and tack them in place. Embroider only to within 5 mm (¼ in) of the outside edges of the collage. Run-stitch patterns using different thicknesses of thread, such as one or more strands of cotton or silk and perle threads equal to numbers 8 and 12. If desired experiment with other threads.

Decorate some of the edges of the collaged fabrics with straight stitches (B in diagram). These may be equal or random lengths, perpendicular or diagonal to the edge of the fabric. Add beads and/or sequins in patterns.

### finishing
Make 4 loops (H in diagram), approximately 7 cm (3 in) long out of the same fabric as the backing, or from bought cord.

Cut off excess muslin around the edges and apply the collage with tacking stitches to the centre of the backing fabric, 40 cm (15 ¾ in) square (I in diagram), to create the front of the article. Join the front and back together by pinning and tacking the other 40 cm (15 ¾ in) square (back of article) to the front, right sides facing each other, and attach the loops to each corner, with 1.5 cm (⅝ in) of the loop pointed towards the centre of the square. Leave an opening of 8 cm (3 ⅛ in) on one side to turn them right side out after machine stitching. Refer to the bagging method of making up book pages in Project 19 'Concertina stitch book'.

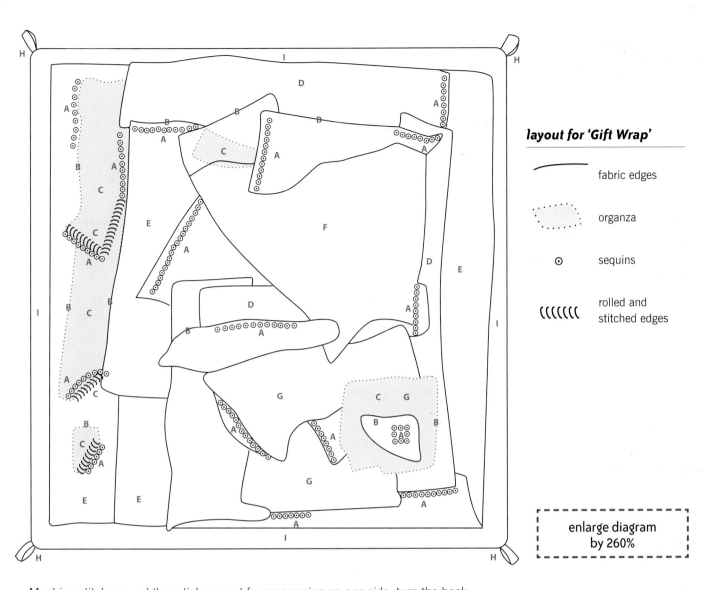

## layout for 'Gift Wrap'

——————— fabric edges

organza

⊙ sequins

((((((( rolled and stitched edges

enlarge diagram by 260%

Machine stitch around the article except for an opening on one side, turn the back and front right side out and press. Close the gap with ladder stitch. Press, and make a line of running stitch 3 mm (1/8 in) away from the edge of the article.

## tufting

To hold the back and front together, tie them with thread and a bead at the back, making five ties on each of five rows (25 ties altogether), 6 cm (2 ⅜ in) apart. Cut 25 x 20 cm (8 in) lengths of perle 8 or other yarn and stitch them through from the back and into the lining (not to the front collage) and out to the back again, making a back stitch 5 mm (¼ in) long in the middle of the thread so that the two tails of thread are even. Refer to the photo showing the corner turned back. Thread a medium sized bead onto one of the tails and tie the two tails together with two overhand knots. Make two more back stitches with the tails and trim the ends to a finished length of approximately 4 cm (1 ½ in).

## cord

Thread either a beaded and wrapped cord or other cord approximately 1.6 m (63 in) long through the four corner loops, stitch the ends together and add beaded pendants to make a tassel. Medium sized round beads are threaded into the core and spaced 5 cm (2 in) apart.

*Detail of straight stitch vertical rows with tight tension*

# colour wash textile herringbone stitch

Create a designer textile to make into an object or article such as a vest-front, clothing detail, bag, cushion or panel.

## finished size of textile approx 30 x 28 cm (11 ¾ x 11 in)

## materials

Create your own colour palette.

■ Indian muslin, 32 x 30 cm (13 ¾ x 11 ¾ in): 1, 2 or more layers depending on the weight of the muslin and your preference; zigzag stitch or overlock the edges together before attaching to the frame (first layer/lining)

■ Silk dupion, organza or other suitable fabric, cut or torn strips, for the background (second layer)

■ Silk dupion, organza or other suitable fabrics for the 9 collaged squares, each 6 cm (2 ⅜ in) square (third layer)

■ Organza fabric, cut or torn strips (fourth layer) placed over the nine squares

■ Embroidery threads: stranded cotton and/or silk

■ Ribbons, silk embroidery 4 mm (3/16 in)

■ Sewing cotton or 1 strand embroidery cotton for tacking

■ Embroidery frame, 30.5 cm (12 in) or

■ Embroidery hoop, 15–18 cm (6–7 in)

■ Pins

■ Needles: embroidery, assorted sizes 3 to 9 or larger as needed

*If you wish, you can experiment with the method by working one section of the design and making it into a 'book page' following the measurements from other projects, and the diagram of the middle square in the top row, which is stitched with Colour Streams 4 mm ribbon Uluru, and DMC stranded cottons 3855 yellow, 223 and 758 pink.*

The background is made with horizontal silk and organza strips, as described in *Project 1*, and the applied squares are similar to those in *Project 3*. Herringbone stitch is shown in *Project 1* as a linear stitch to decorate and

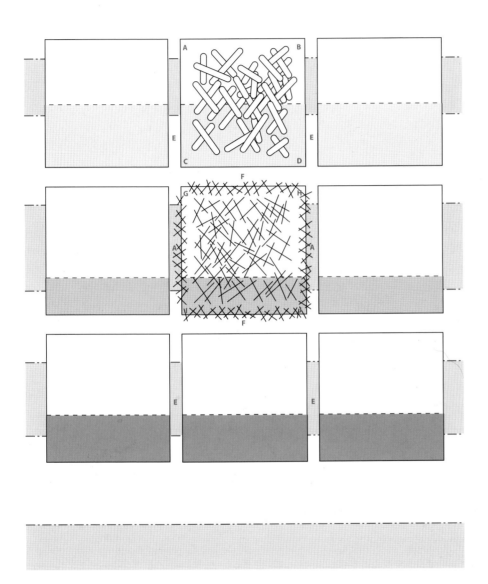

### layout for the whole panel

— - — · — · —
second layer, background strips

——————
third layer, squares

fourth layer, organza strips, lightest
tonal value

fourth layer, organza strips, medium
tonal value

fourth layer, organza strips, dark
tonal value

enlarge diagram
by 230%

secure edges of fabric. In this project, however, herringbone stitch is used as a
space filler to attach and blend edges of fabric and in stitching freely across the
surface in colours that create light and dark contrasts of shading.

Rather than working herringbone stitch in evenly spaced, straight lines, this
project and *Project 6 'Butterflies out of a box'* explore a softer, more organic
effect with shading made by overlapping irregular, random stitches.

In *Project 6* herringbone stitch is applied in concentric circles to create
movement as well as shading.

Both projects explore light and dark tonal contrasts by combining embroidery
ribbon, and stranded cottons and silks, in layers to achieve a surface similar to a
painted wash of colour.

*Detail of middle square, top row.*

## method

Collage the strips of silk dupion and organza (second layer) horizontally, overlapping edges 1 cm (⅜ in) onto muslin (first layer), for a finished size of 30 x 28 (11 ¾ x 11 in), and tack into place.

Pin and tack nine 6 cm (2 ⅜ in) squares A-B-C-D (third layer) onto the second layer, spacing them 5 mm (¼ in) apart vertically, E, and horizontally, F, as per diagram.

Tack and run-stitch strips of organza on top of the nine squares as indicated by the shaded areas in the diagram (fourth layer).

Within each square work random herringbone and cross stitches with 4 mm (³⁄₁₆ in) silk ribbon, an example shown in A-B-C-D, then work another layer of random herringbone stitches over the ribbon with one strand of cotton or silk, examples shown in G-H-I-J and photo detail.

Work random herringbone stitches along the edges of the strips made in the second layer.

If you like the effect I have achieved here, choose your colours so that the tonal values are graded from dark to medium to light from left to right across each horizontal row, and vertically from predominantly light on the top row to medium in the middle row and dark in the bottom row.

*A tip on applying colours: to grade them gradually by tonal value, use some of the same colours from the lightest and darkest squares in the middle square.*

Work herringbone stitch around the edges of the squares and the background strips, embroidering only to within 5 mm (¼ in) of the outside edges of the collage.

## colours used

**row 1**  Colour Streams 4 mm ribbon Uluru
*Left*: DMC 3827 yellow, 223 and 3722 pink
*Centre*: DMC 3855 yellow, 223 and 758 pink
*Right*: DMC 758 pink, 3827 and 3855 yellow.

**row 2**  Colour Streams 4 mm ribbon Lilli Pilli
*Left*: DMC 3820 yellow, 581 yellow-green, 3726 pink
*Centre*: DMC 753 green, 316 pink, 3820 yellow
*Right*: DMC 734 green, 758 pink, 3046 yellow.

**row 3**  Colour Streams 4 mm ribbon Arabian Nights
*Left*: DMC 3834 violet, 3809 blue, 581 yellow-green
*Centre*: 3835 violet, 3848 blue-green, 733 yellow-green
*Right*: 3836 pink, 3849 blue-green, 734 yellow-green.

# butterflies out of a box
## herringbone & cross stitch colour wash (book page)

Layers of cross stitch and herringbone stitches are applied to a fabric collage background to create movement and shading reminiscent of a colour wash.

Rhythm and movement are created by applying the stitches in ribbon and embroidery thread in five concentric, almost circular rows. Two wrapped cords are applied and overstitched with raised close plaited herringbone and Vandyke stitch. The finished collage is applied to another fabric and made into a page for Project 19, 'Concertina stitch book'.

## method

Collage small scraps of squares and rectangles of silk dupion (second layer) overlapping edges 1 cm (⅜ in) in a harmonious colour range (I used orange/red, red and magenta) onto muslin (first layer/lining), for a finished size of 11.5 cm (4 ½ in) to 12 cm (4 ¾ in) approximately square.

Attach the collage pieces with small running stitches in 1 strand matching cotton, 3 mm (⅛ in) in from the edges. Embroider only to within 5 mm (¼ in) of the outside edges of the collage. Transfer the design by tacking the guidelines for the herringbone stitches (diagram A) and placement of the cords (diagram B). Work different sizes of random cross stitch with 4 mm (³⁄₁₆ in) embroidery

**finished size of collage approx 11.5 cm to 12 cm (4 ½ in to 4 ¾ in) square**

### materials
Create your own palette of colours.

■ Indian muslin 25 cm (9 ⅞ in) square: 1, 2 or more layers depending on the weight of the muslin and your preference; zigzag stitch or overlock the edges together before attaching to a frame (first layer/lining)

■ Silk dupion and organza scraps and strips for the background (second layer)

■ Embroidery threads, stranded cotton and/or silk: I used Colour Streams Silken Strands in Umbrian Gold, Uluru, Mardi Gras and Straw, and approximately 10 m (11 yds) DMC stranded cotton 783 for the wrapped cords

■ Silk embroidery ribbon: 4 mm (³⁄₁₆ in); I used Colour Streams 4 mm in Lilli Pilli, Straw, Plum, Uluru

■ Metallic thread equal to perle 5 in thickness, such as Madeira 9803/3008 (refer to General Hints in Section 8 for preventing frayed ends)

■ Clear adhesive fabric or craft glue

■ Sewing cotton or 1 strand embroidery cotton for tacking

■ Embroidery frame, 30.5 cm (12 in) or

■ Embroidery hoop, 15–18 cm (6–7 in)

■ Pins

■ Needles: embroidery, assorted sizes 3 to 7 or larger as needed

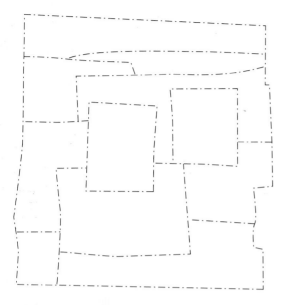

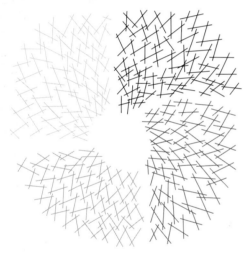

ribbon, leaving gaps in the 'concentric circles' as indicated in diagram B. Work rows of herringbone stitch, overlapping each other, on top of the ribbon and continuing the lines of the 'concentric circles' with 1 strand cotton or silk. Refer to the photo of the finished project.

Make two wrapped cords without the bead string (see Section 5, Cords for embellishment and trimming) and compress them for a stiffer, smoother line. The finished horizontal wrapped cord is 20 cm (8 in) long with a 2 cm (¾ in) tassel at each end. The core consists of 12 x 33 cm (13 in) lengths of stranded cotton and one wrapping thread 1.5 m (60 in) long. Wrap for 20 cm (8 in), and trim the ends to leave a 2 cm (¾ in) tassel. The finished vertical wrapped cord is 12.5 cm (4 $^{15}/_{16}$ in). The core consists of 12 x 22 cm (8 ⅝ in) lengths of stranded cotton and one wrapping thread 1.5 m (60 in) long. Wrap for 12.5 cm (4 $^{15}/_{16}$ in), and trim the ends to leave a 2 cm (¾ in) tassel.

Tie a loose overhand knot in the centre of the horizontal wrapped cord and stitch the cord in place with 1 strand matching thread. Slip the vertical wrapped cord through the centre of the overhand knot and couch it in place. The vertical wrapped cord is overstitched with overlapping herringbone stitch, and the horizontal cord with Vandyke stitch, both in metallic thread. Cut off excess muslin and make the embroidered collage into a book page as shown for Project 19.

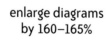

enlarge diagrams by 160–165%

*Top*: Layout for collaged background see also photo 'Red patches' on page 23.
*Above*: Radiating patterns created in herringbone stitch in 1 strand cotton or silk
*Right: Diagram A*
Guidelines for placement of herringbone stitches
*Far right: Diagram B*
Position of wrapped cords among ribbon cross stitches (for simplicity the herringbone stitches in embroidery thread are omitted)

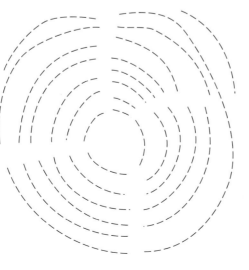

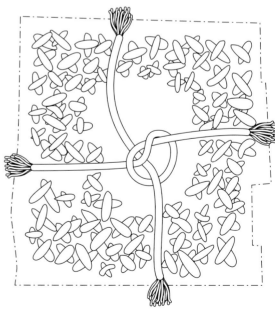

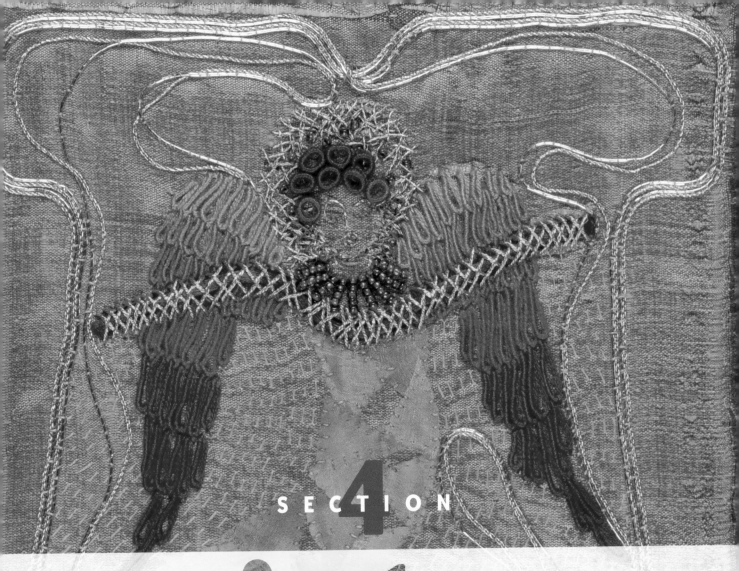

SECTION 4

# stitches
## for colour & effect

Create beautiful textures and effects using stitches, wrapping, beads, chopped silk, metallic threads, cords, and folded and pleated ribbons and organza

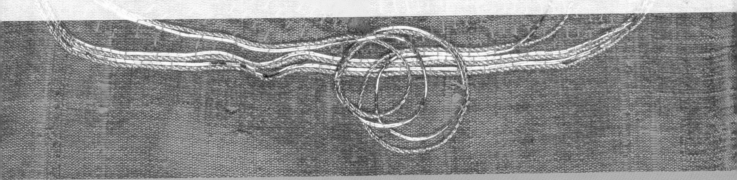

# knotty waves

raised chain band and wave stitch panel (book page)

Raised chain band is a wonderful composite textured stitch which has many applications as an isolated, linear or filling stitch. Wave stitch was historically used in straight, even rows, with small stitches, to fill shapes such as leaves and petals in nineteenth century white work.

**finished size of book page collage approx 11.5 to 12 cm (4 ½ in to 4 ¾ in) square**

## materials

■ Create your own palette of colours.

Indian muslin, 25 cm (9 ⅞ in) square: 1, 2 or more layers depending on the weight of the muslin and your preference; zigzag stitch or overlock the edges together before attaching to a frame (first layer/lining)

■ Silk dupion for the background (second layer)

■ Embroidery threads: silk and cotton equal to perle 3, 5 and 8, stranded cotton

■ Silk embroidery ribbon, 4 mm (³⁄₁₆ in)

■ Metallic thread equal to perle 8 in thickness such as Madeira metallic 9803/3008 and 9805/5012 (see p 121 to prevent frayed ends)

■ Clear adhesive fabric or craft glue

■ Beads, bugle 2.5 cm (1 in) long

Beading needle

■ Beading thread (or size 50 sewing cotton pulled through beeswax)

■ Sewing cotton or 1 strand embroidery cotton for tacking

■ Embroidery frame, 30.5 cm (12 in) or

■ Embroidery hoop, 15–18 cm (6–7 in)

■ Pins

■ Needles: embroidery, assorted sizes 3 to 7 or larger as needed

It is very effective when the scale is enlarged and the stitches worked randomly, unevenly, and in wavy rows. Textured and organic patterns are created when raised chains are worked on the straight arms of wave stitch, and different textures and thicknesses of thread such as embroidery ribbon, metallic and perle threads are used.

Here we explore many variations of raised chain band and wave stitch as a book page on a collage of fabrics.

The finished collage is applied to another fabric and made into a page for the concertina stitch book of Project 19.

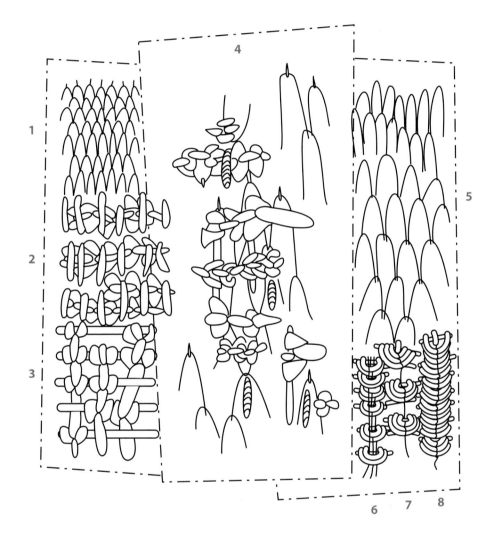

1 Evenly worked straight rows of wave stitch

2 Horizontal rows of raised chain band worked in silk ribbon overstitched with running stitch

3 Vertical rows of raised chain band worked over bugle beads in knitting yarn

4 Large uneven wave stitches worked randomly with metallic thread equal to perle 5, raised chain band in silk ribbon and thread, and scattered bullion stitches

5 Wave stitch worked in perle 5 in uneven rows

6 Raised chain band worked three times over one foundation bar in metallic thread equal to perle 8 (9805/4012)

7 Raised chain band worked three times over two foundation bars in metallic thread equal to perle 5 (9803/3008)

8 Raised chain band worked three times over one foundation bar in metallic thread equal to perle 5 (9803/3008)

## method

Collage the silk dupion (second layer), overlapping edges 1 cm (⅜ in), onto the muslin lining (first layer), the same size as the finished size given and tack into place. Attach the silk pieces with small running stitches in 1 strand matching cotton, 3 mm (⅛ in) in from the edges. Embroider only to within 5 mm (¼ in) of the outside edges of the collage.

Stitch patterns of wave stitch and raised chain band using the photo and diagram as guides.

Cut off excess muslin and make the embroidered collage into a book page as shown in Project 19.

# chequerboard wrapped stitches panel
finished with a wrapped and knotted cord with seashell 'beads'

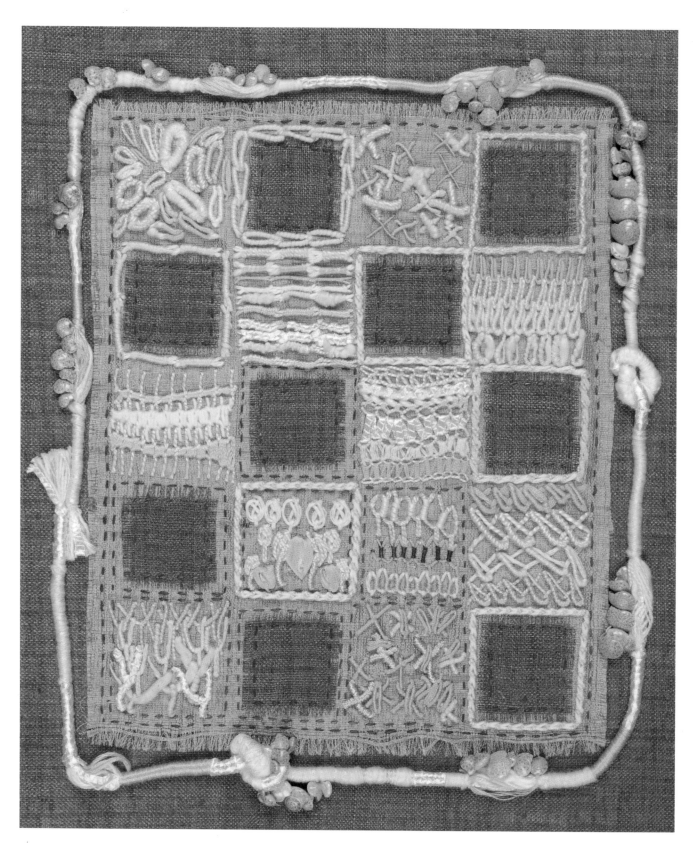

This panel experiments with wrapping all or part of traditional stitches, worked in different thicknesses and textures of threads, to add a smooth surface to contrast with the pattern made by the stitches.

Stitches worked in neutral shades of white, off-white, cream and beige are enhanced by applied squares of terracotta-coloured raw silk in all but one of the alternate squares of a chequerboard framework, producing a dramatic light/dark tonal contrast. Other colours which complement the neutral threads may be used for the backgrounds and applied squares. A large variety of textures and weights of threads such as crochet, knitting and weaving yarns is readily available in neutral colours.

A muslin lining is not used in this project. The stitches are worked on two layers of fabric—the first layer is a background of terracotta raw silk, the second layer is beige raw silk, the third layer is small squares of terracotta raw silk, the same as the first layer, applied in all but one of the empty spaces.

Frame the finished panel, or make it into a bag, book cover or cushion enhanced with a wrapped and knotted cord using seashell 'beads', a perfect frame for natural threads and raw silk fabrics.

## method

Attach terracotta background fabric 36 x 30 (14 ⅛ x 11 ¾ in) (first layer) to frame. Pin and tack beige fabric 21 x 17.5 cm (8 ¼ x 6 ⅞ in) (second layer) to the centre of the first layer. Transfer the design to the fabric.

Pin and tack the nine 3 cm (1 ³⁄₁₆ in) terracotta squares into position and run-stitch them with 3 strands cotton or silk in a matching colour, as shown in diagram and photo.

Run stitch around some of the stitched squares and the outside border in the same colour, as shown in diagram and photo.

Work stitches in the eleven beige squares as described in the caption to the diagram.

**finished size of panel**
**27 x 23.5 cm (10 ⅝ x 9 ¼ in)**

### materials

■ Terracotta silk dupion or raw silk background, 36 x 30 (14 ⅛ x 11 ¾ in), zigzag stitch or overlock the edges before attaching to a frame (first layer)

■ Beige silk dupion or raw silk with raw edges slightly frayed, 21 x 17.5 cm (8 ¼ x 6 ⅞ in) (second layer)

■ Terracotta silk dupion or raw silk for appliqué, 9 pieces 3 cm (1 ³⁄₁₆ in) square (third layer)

■ Embroidery threads: silk, linen and cotton equal to perle 3, 5 and 8, stranded cotton, other suitable yarns and ribbon

■ Threads and/or yarns for wrapped and beaded cord

■ Beads or shells with holes for wrapped and beaded cord

■ Beading needle

■ Beading thread (or size 50 sewing cotton pulled through beeswax)

■ Sewing cotton or 1 strand cotton for tacking

■ Embroidery frame, 30.5 cm (12 in) or to suit size of project

■ Pins

■ Needles: embroidery, assorted sizes 1 to 7 or larger as needed; tapestry sizes 16–24 or larger as needed

## *embroidery guide for* **Chequerboard**

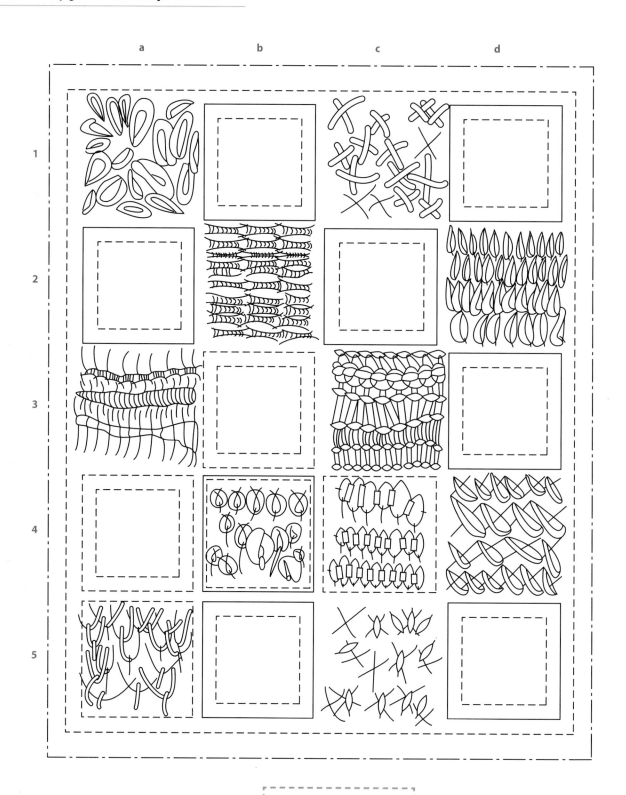

enlarge diagram
by 145%

## embroidery guide

### row 1

**a** Chain stitch, detached and wrapped

**b** Border of chain stitch, wrapped

**c** Cross stitch, wrapped

**d** Border of chain stitch, each chain whipped three times

### row 2

**a** Border of fancy hem stitch

**b** Fancy hem stitch

**c** Border of chain stitch, whipped

**d** Chain stitch of varying sizes, detached and wrapped on one side

### row 3

**a** Two rows of blanket stitch worked back-to-back and then wrapped together

**b** No extra stitches are worked in this box

**c** Two rows of chain stitch wrapped together five times

**d** Border of chain stitch, whipped

### row 4

**a** No extra stitches are worked in this box

**b** Chain stitch, oyster variation

**c** Three rows of chain stitch, detached, side-by-side and wrapped together

**d** Cross stitch, chained, wrapped on one side

### row 5

**a** Fly stitch, wrapped

**b** No extra stitches are worked in this box

**c** Cross stitch, wrapped and overlapped with chain, detached and wrapped

**d** Border of chain stitch, whipped

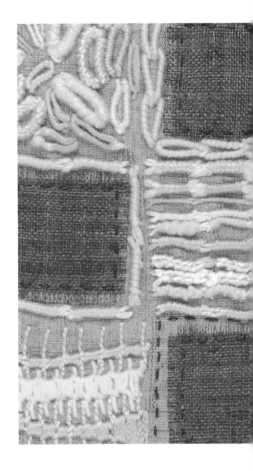

Frame the completed embroidery or make it up into a panel or other article with a beaded and wrapped cord made on a core equal to 12 to 15 lengths of 6 stranded cotton, with decorative seashells or beads attached, and approximately 85 cm (33 ½ in) long, long enough to allow for two overhand knots to be tied. Attach the cord to the panel with matching cotton.

# bushfire wrapped stitches (book page)

Wrapped stitches, previously encountered in separate one-stitch groups in Project 8 'Chequerboard', are brought together in this design, translating the wild colours of an Australian bushfire into the vibrant deep warm colours of silk and cotton threads on a space-dyed background of silk habutai.

**finished size for book page collage approx 11.5 cm to 12 cm (4 ½ in to 4 ¾ in) square**

### materials

Create your own palette of colours.

■ Indian muslin, 25 cm (9 ⅞ in) square: 1, 2 or more layers depending on the weight of the muslin and your preference; zigzag stitch or overlock the edges together before attaching to a frame (first layer/lining)

■ Silk dupion or silk habutai for the background (second layer); Colour Streams space-dyed silk habutai 'Venetian Sunset' used here

■ Embroidery threads: stranded silk and cotton, and silk and cotton equal to perle 3, 5 and 8

■ Ribbon, silk embroidery, 4 mm (³/₁₆ in); Colour Streams 'Venetian Sunset' used here

■ Metallic thread equal to perle 8 and 12 in thickness such as Madeira 9803/3008 and 9805/3007

■ Clear adhesive fabric or craft glue

■ Sewing cotton or 1 strand embroidery cotton for tacking

■ Embroidery frame, 30.5 cm (12 in), or

■ Embroidery hoop, 15–18 cm (6–7 in)

■ Pins

■ Needles: embroidery, assorted sizes 3 to 7 or larger as needed

The finished collage is applied to another fabric and made into a page for the concertina stitch book shown in Project 19.

### method

Collage the silk dupion, overlapping edges 1 cm (⅜ in) (second layer) onto muslin (first layer/lining) the same size as the finished size given. Attach them with small running stitches in 1 strand matching cotton 3 mm (⅛ in) in from the edges of each scrap. Embroider only to within 5 mm (1/4 in) of the outside edges of the collage.

First work the random cross stitches, 1 in diagram A, with silk embroidery ribbon. Then, guided by diagram B, work the herringbone stitches (2) in one strand of silk thread, using the diagram and photo as guides. Then work the other embroidery stitches: fancy hem (3); wrapped straight and cross stitches (4); detached chain

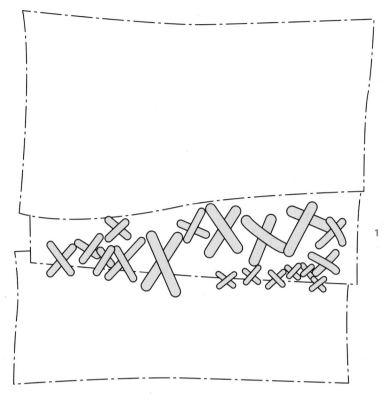

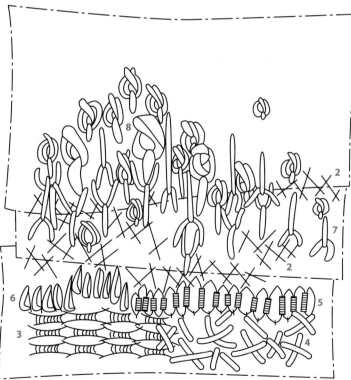

### Diagram A

*Layout for background collage of three strips selectively cut and torn from space-dyed silk habutai, and suggested positions for the ribbon cross stitches.*

### Diagram B

**2** herringbone stitch

**3** fancy hem

**4** wrapped straight and cross stitches

**5** detached chain stitch, sides wrapped together

**6** detached chain stitch one half wrapped

**7** fly and wrapped fly

**8** oyster chain variation

```
enlarge diagrams
by 120–125%
```

stitch, sides wrapped together (5); detached chain stitch, one half wrapped (6); fly and wrapped fly stitch (7); and oyster chain variation (8).

Cut off excess muslin and make the embroidered collage into a book page as shown in Project 19.

# turquoise & yellow bullion stitch panel or bag

Bullion stitch is one of the most beautiful and versatile of textured and raised stitches. It looks wonderful on its own or blended with others.

In this project a background fabric is divided into squares with knitting ribbon in a toning colour. Unevenly shaped shapes of turquoise silk are frayed and applied with running stitch in alternate squares. Variations of bullion stitch are used in the remaining squares, in all but one also attaching a piece of metallic twisted cord.

Create your own panel or bag based on this model, or a book page of just four squares, using the fabrics and threads available to you.

## method

Attach background fabric, ribbon and uneven shapes of silk to muslin lining (first layer) and tack and stitch into place, the same size as the finished size given. Make small running stitches in 1 strand cotton 3 mm (⅛ in) in from the edges of the uneven shapes.

Embroider only to within 5 mm (¼ in) of the outside edges of the fabric. Attach metallic twisted cords.

Stitch all bullion stitches with milliners/straw needles as follows using the diagram and photo as guides.

### row 1

**b** *top* Zigzag pattern of bullion stitches with stranded cotton over metallic cord.
below Zigzag braid, worked with stranded cotton, bottom row worked first:
line 6: 6 strands, 18 wraps, size 1 needle
line 5: 5 strands, 18 wraps, size 3 needle
line 4: 4 strands, 20 wraps, size 5 needle
line 3: 3 strands, 20 wraps, size 5–7 needle
line 2: 2 strands, 22 wraps, size 5–7 needle
line 1: 1 strand 25 wraps size 7–9 needle

### row 2

**a** *top* Linked bullion stitch, 4 strands cotton, 18 wraps, size 3 needle.
*below* Linked bullion stitch, same as above, over the piece of metallic cord.

**c** Linked bullion in stranded cotton with raised chain band worked with metallic thread on the links and over the piece of metallic cord.

### row 3

**b** Long-armed bullion stitches, worked in various threads including metallic.

finished size of panel 22 x 17 cm (8 5/8 in x 6 11/16 in)

## materials
Create your own palette of colours.

- Indian muslin, 27 x 22 cm (10 ⅝ x 8 ⅝ in): 1, 2 or more layers depending on the weight of the muslin and your preference; zigzag stitch or overlock the edges together before attaching to a frame (first layer/lining)

- Indian muslin, 25 cm (9 ⅞ in) square

- Silk dupion or raw silk, 25 x 20 cm (9 ⅞ in x 8 in) for the background (second layer)

- Ribbon, silk or knitting, to divide background into sections (second layer)

- Embroidery threads, stranded cotton, silk and perle (I used DMC stranded colours 783 yellow, 597 turquoise blue, 3843 and 3845 peacock blue)

- Silk dupion or habutai, six uneven shapes for panel

- Cord, twisted metallic 4 mm (³/₁₆ in) in diameter

- Metallic thread equal to perle 8 in thickness, such as Madeira 7805/5105

- Clear adhesive fabric or craft glue to seal ends of metallic cords and threads

- Sewing cotton or 1 strand embroidery cotton for tacking

- Embroidery frame, 30.5 cm (12 in), or

- Embroidery hoop, 15–18 cm (6–7 in)

- Pins

- Needles: embroidery, assorted sizes 3 to 7 or larger as needed

- milliners/straw sizes 1 and 3

a b c

## layout and stitch guide
## for bullion stitch panel

ribbon

silk

metallic cords

enlarge diagram
by 175%

1

2

3

4

### row 4

**a** Crossed bullion stitches, various sizes and threads including metallic, some over the piece of metallic cord.

**c** Bullion stitches tied off with a chain stitch. From left to right, bullion stitches are made with 14, 16, 18, 20, 18, 16 and 14 wraps, using six strands cotton and a size 1 needle.

Cut off excess muslin, fringe the edges and make the collage into a panel, bag or book page. Finish off with a wrapped cord and knotted pendant tassels.

# colour, texture & pattern bullion stitch panel

This panel, which may be mounted or made into a bag, includes many variations of geometric and floral patterns enhanced with cords, beads and metallic threads stitched onto a collage of silk strips, their edges decorated with vertical straight stitches.

Bullion stitch is one of the most beautiful and versatile of textured and raised stitches. It looks wonderful on its own or blended with others.

## method

Attach strips of background fabric onto muslin (first layer/lining), overlapping edges 1 cm (⅜ in) and tack and stitch into place, the same size as the finished size given.

Embroider only to within 5 mm (¼ in) of the outside edges of the fabric.

All the edges of the strips are overstitched with vertical straight stitches in perle 5 and 8.

Work the patterns as follows using the diagram and photo as guides. All needles specified for bullion stitches are milliners/straw.

**finished size of collage
25 x 16 cm (9 7/8 in x 6 ¼ in)**

## materials

Create your own palette of colours.

■ Indian muslin, 30 cm (11 ¾ in) x 23 cm (9 in): 1, 2 or more layers depending on the weight of the muslin and your preference: zigzag stitch or overlock the edges together before attaching to a frame (first layer/lining)

■ Silk dupion or raw silk strips of different widths for the background (second layer)

■ Embroidery threads: stranded silk or cotton, perle 5 and 8, stranded cotton (I used DMC stranded cotton in colours 3854 yellow orange, 351 pink, 402 apricot, 3804 pink, 977 yellow ochre medium, 3827 yellow ochre, 921 terracotta medium, 3849 aqua, 3746 blue violet, 718 magenta; Needle Necessities space-dyed stranded cotton, red/orange/violet; perle 5 and 8 for vertical straight stitches on edges of strips; perle 5 for fly stitches in row 4)

■ Metallic thread equal to perle 8 in thickness, such as Madeira 7803/3007

■ Cord, twisted or flat braided metallic

■ Clear adhesive fabric or craft glue

■ Beads, assorted sizes and shapes, small and medium round and bugle

**materials** continued page 58>

*layout guide for stitches*

enlarge diagram by 110 %

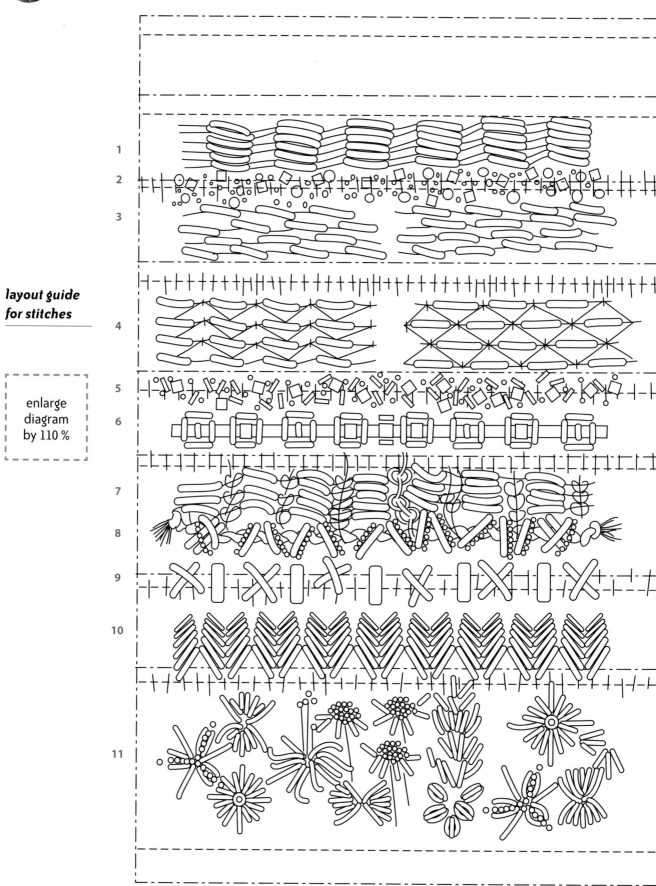

# folded & pleated ribbons
## with beads and stitches (book page)

Here folded and pleated ribbons are enhanced by adding beads and stitches.
Different effects can be created depending on the nature of the ribbons—whether
they are stiff and firm, soft and silky, or transparent and filmy.

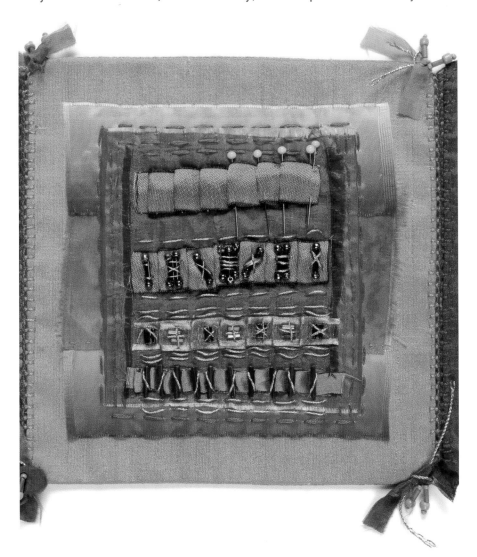

**finished size for book page collage approx 11.5 to 12 cm (4 ½ in to 4 ¾ in) square**

### materials
Create your own palette of colours.

■ Indian muslin, 25 cm (9 ⅞ in) square: 1, 2 or more layers depending on the weight of the muslin and your preference; zigzag stitch or overlock the edges together before attaching to a frame (first layer/lining)

■ Silk dupion for the background (second layer)

■ Embroidery threads: stranded cotton or silk

■ Ribbons, 1.5 cm (⅝ in), 1 cm (⅜ in), 8 mm (⁵⁄₁₆ in) wide (if you see a desirable wire-edged ribbon, remember you can remove the wire)

■ Metallic gold twist thread

■ Metallic thread equal to perle 8 in thickness such as Madeira 9803/3007

■ Clear adhesive fabric or craft glue

■ Beads: bugle, medium 6 mm (¼ in) and medium/long 12 mm (½ in); small round dress; square, rectangular or other

■ Beading needle

■ Beading thread (or size 50 sewing cotton pulled through beeswax)

■ Sewing cotton or 1 strand embroidery cotton for tacking

■ Embroidery frame, 30.5 cm (12 in), or

■ Embroidery hoop 15–18 cm (6–7 in)

■ Pins

■ Needles: embroidery, assorted sizes 3 to 7 or larger as needed

Rows of running stitch in metallic thread between the ribbons create a braid-like quality. Richly embroidered areas are created where spaces are filled with multiple rows of folded and pleated ribbons alternating with running stitches in metallic thread, and attractive borders when applied as one, two or more lines. The pins in the first row are only there to illustrate the method of folding the ribbon; they are removed after the ribbon has been stitched.

Create a book page following this step-by-step project. You could also use it as the basis for another book page, adapting sections of the next project, 'Ancient Eyes'.

The finished collage is applied to another fabric and made into a book page for Project 19.

### method

Collage the silk dupion, overlapping edges 1 cm (⅜ in) (second layer) onto muslin (first layer/lining), the same size as the finished size given, and tack into place. Attach the pieces with small running stitches in 1 strand matching cotton, 3 mm (⅛ in) in from the edges. Embroider only to within 5 mm (¼ in) of the outside edges of the collage.

Work the patterns as follows using the photo as a guide:

### row 1

Pin 1.5 cm (⅝ in) wide ribbon into place, allowing 2 cm (¾ in) to start, then folding back 1 cm (⅜ in) and folding forward 2 cm (¾ in); repeat to the end. These measurements may be varied for different effects. Stitch the folds into place at each pin with matching sewing or embroidery cotton.

### row 2

Fold and pleat ribbon 1 cm (⅜ in) wide and decorate it with bead patterns 'captured' with stitches made with metallic thread.

### row 3

Fold and pleat the bordered ribbon 1 cm (⅜ in) wide and decorate it with bead patterns 'captured' with stitches made with metallic thread.

### row 4

Fold and pleat soft ribbon 8 mm (⁵⁄₁₆ in) wide and decorate it with bugle beads 'captured' with straight stitches.

Cut off excess muslin and make the embroidered collage into a book page for Project 19.

# ancient eyes
## folded and pleated ribbons with beads and stitches

This project features folded and pleated ribbons and beads captured
with metallic threads, metallic cords overstitched with bullions and beads,
straight stitches, chopped silk and couched metallic threads.

**finished size of panel**
**30 x 24 cm (11 ¾ x 9 ½ in)**

### materials
Create your own palette of colours.

■ Indian muslin, 30 x 27 cm (11 ¾ x
10 ⅝ in): 1, 2 or more layers depending
on the weight of the muslin and your
preference; zigzag stitch or overlock
the edges together before attaching to
a frame (first layer/lining)

■ Silk dupion, organza and/or other
rich fabrics, 1 piece for background 30
x 24 cm (11 ¾ x 9 ½ in), other pieces
for collage (second layer and chopped
silk, refer to page 68 for chopped silk
instructions)

■ Embroidery threads: stranded
cottons for bullion stitches and any
other suitable threads

■ Ribbons: metallic 1 cm (⅜ in) and 4
cm (1 ½ in) wide; soft ribbon 12 mm
(½ in); organza ribbon 2.5 cm (1 in)
wide

■ Metallic threads equal to perle
8 in thickness, such as Madeira
9803/3008, gold check, imitation
Japanese gold, gold twist or other

■ Cords, metallic, twisted, different
widths, and flat braid

■ Clear adhesive fabric or craft glue
and cords

■ Sewing silk or stranded cotton,

**materials** continued over page >

Make one or two panels of 'Ancient Eyes' using this example as a starting point,
or experiment with the method by making a 'book page' of selected sections and
following the measurements from other projects.

### method
Collage silk dupion, overlapping edges 1 cm (⅜ in) (second layer) onto muslin
(first layer/lining), the same size as the finished size given, and tack into place.

## ancient eyes

### materials continued

- Beading needle

- Beading thread (or size 50 sewing cotton pulled through beeswax)

- Sewing cotton or 1 strand embroidery cotton for tacking

- Embroidery frame, 30.5 cm (12 in), or

- Embroidery hoop, 15–18 cm (6–7 in)

- Needles: embroidery, assorted sizes 1 to 9 or larger as needed; tapestry, sizes 18 to 24 or larger as needed; milliners/straw, size 1 and 3

- Pins

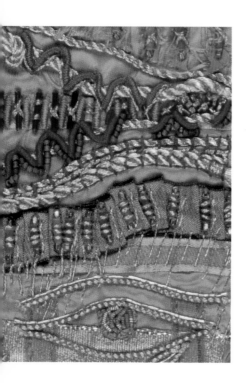

Attach pieces with small running stitches in 1 strand matching cotton 3 mm (⅛ in) in from the edges. Embroider only to within 5 mm (¼ in) of the outside edges of the collage.

Transfer the designs from the layout guide to the fabric.

Attach all ribbons and cords.

Work stitches and beading using the photo and diagram as guides.

### left panel

Embellished ribbons and cords. Note: The eye, 10, is stitched first.

**1** Bullion stitches over metallic cord.

**2** Chopped silk decorated with a bugle bead with two round beads at each end captured with cross stitches in thick metallic thread.

**3** Metallic cord stitched to fabric.

**4** Bullion stitches and straight stitches in thick metallic thread over metallic cord.

**5** Bullion stitches alternating with bugle beads captured with cross and straight stitches on ribbon.

**6** Zigzag line of bullion stitches and strings of beads over metallic cord.

**7** Blanket stitch over two metallic cords, wrapped together with thick gold thread.

**8** Folded ribbon 12 mm (½ in) wide, each fold applied with a bugle bead with two round beads at each end captured with straight stitches, and straight stitches on each fold in thick metallic thread.

**9** Slanted straight stitches in thin and thick metallic thread over ribbon.

**10** Outline of eye and eyebrow is made by attaching thin cord and couching imitation Japanese gold alongside each other. The eyeball is made with French knots and gold check. Bugle and round beads are applied diagonally in vertical lines on either side of the eye.

**11** Imitation Japanese gold thread twisted around a finger is randomly stitched onto the background and diagonal straight stitches worked over the top.

**12** Zigzag lines of bullion stitches and strings of small round beads are made over the top of thick metallic cord.

### right panel

Metallic threads, cords and ribbons are applied to a collage of fabric.

**13** Worked first, the eye is made of twisted metallic cords and imitation Japanese gold; below it are three vertical lines of narrow ribbon overstitched with medium sized bugle beads applied diagonally. The eyeball is made from bugle and round beads.

**14** Three layers of meandering lines of metallic threads, gold twist, copper, and imitation Japanese gold, are couched over each other.

**15** Soft organza ribbon 25 mm (1 in) wide is folded in pleats and stitched down on the edges. A line of fine metallic thread meanders across the folds. At

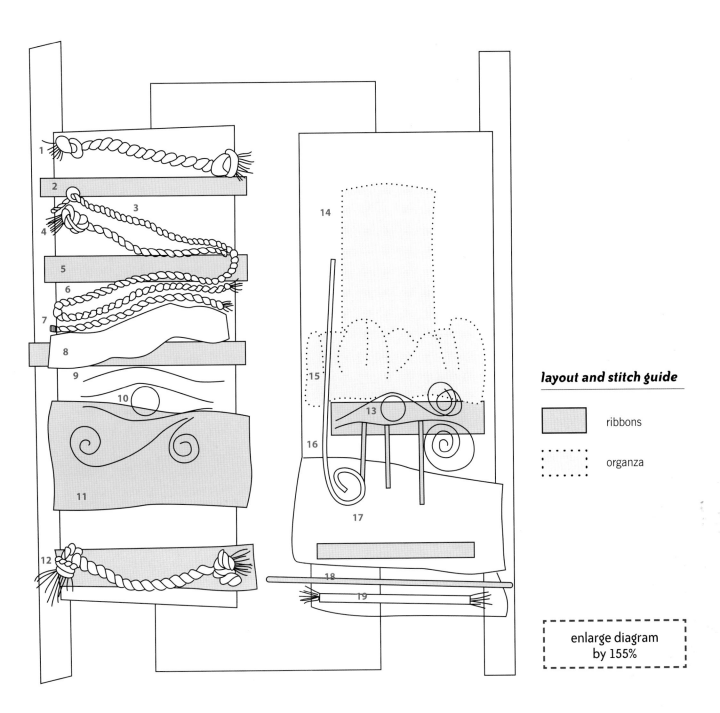

*layout and stitch guide*

ribbons

organza

enlarge diagram
by 155%

the base of the ribbon large and medium round beads, and bugle beads, are applied and overstitched with bullion stitches.

**16** Metallic cord stitched to the background.

**17** Fine metallic thread is couched in a meandering pattern.

**18** Round beads are applied to a narrow ribbon.

**19** Bugle and flat beads are applied onto flat metallic braid.

Make up the finished work into a panel.

# chopped silk, stitches & beads book page

The step-by-step method of making patterns of chopped silk may be made into a page for a concertina stitch book shown in Project 19. It is an opportunity to practice and experiment with different ribbons, beads and stitches.

**finished size for book page collage approx 11.5 cm to 12 cm (4 ½ in to 4 ¾ in) square**

## materials

Create your own palette of colours.

■ Indian muslin, 25 cm (9 ⅞ in) square: 1, 2 or more layers depending on the weight of the muslin and your preference; zigzag stitch or overlock the edges together before attaching to a frame (first layer/lining)

■ Silk dupion for the background (second layer)

■ Silk dupion or silk habutai for chopped silk, strips 1.5 cm (⅝ in) wide

■ Embroidery threads, stranded cotton or silk

■ Metallic thread: equal to perle 8 and 12 in thickness, such as Madeira 9803/3007 and 9805/5012; fine 3-ply such as DMC fil d'or or Butterfly metallic

■ Clear adhesive fabric or craft glue

■ Beads: bugle, short 4 mm (³⁄₁₆ in), medium 6 mm (¼ in), medium-long 12 mm (½ in); small round dress beads

■ Beading needle

■ Beading thread (or size 50 sewing cotton pulled through beeswax)

■ Sewing cotton or 1 strand embroidery cotton for tacking

■ Embroidery frame, 30.5 cm (12 in), or

■ Embroidery hoop, 15–18 cm (6–7 in)

■ Pins

■ Needles: embroidery, assorted sizes 3 to 7 or larger as needed

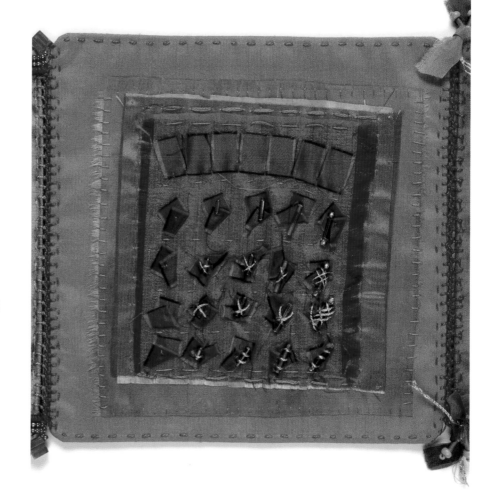

## method

Collage the background with two pieces of silk dupion, overlapping edges 1 cm (⅜ in) (second layer) onto muslin (first layer/lining), the same size as the finished size given, and tack into place. Embroider only to within 5 mm (¼ in) of the outside edges of the collage.

Work the patterns as follows, using the photo as a guide. First, chop the fabric into pieces 1.5 x 1 cm (⅝ x ⅜ in).

**row 1**

A strip of fabric chopped and ready for use.
For each of the following rows, fold five pieces of chopped silk diagonally and, using a beading needle and thread, attach them to the fabric with a small stitch. Leaving the first piece in each row undecorated, add beads and stitches as follows:

**row 2**

**a** Attach a short bugle bead on top of chopped silk with two stitches through each bead.

**b** Attach a medium bugle bead on top of chopped silk with two stitches through each bead.

**c** Attach a medium/long bugle bead on top of chopped silk with two stitches through each bead.

**d** Attach two small round beads at each end of a medium/long bugle bead on top of chopped silk with two stitches through them.

**row 3**

Attach the same size beads as row 2 onto each piece of chopped silk and work cross stitches over them with fine metallic threads.

**row 4**

Same as row 3, but make the cross stitches with medium metallic thread.

**row 5**

Same as row 2, but use straight stitches made with thick metallic thread.
Cut off excess muslin and make the embroidered collage into a book page for Project 19.

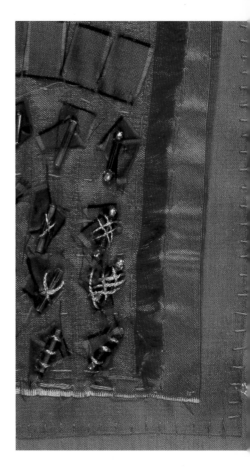

# **butterfly** chopped silk, stitches and beads

A background of collaged silks, including a patterned fabric behind the top of the butterfly, is merged with running stitches, scattered straight stitches and bugle beads, with some of the edges decorated with vertical straight stitches.

**finished size of collage approx 35 x 27 cm (13 ¾ in x 10 5/8 in)**

**materials**

Create your own palette of colours.

■ Indian muslin, 30 x 27 cm (11 ¾ x 10 ⅝ in): 1, 2 or more layers depending on the weight of the muslin and your preference; zigzag stitch or overlock the edges together before attaching to a frame (first layer/lining)

■ Silk dupion and/or other rich fabrics: strips in various widths, 2.5 to 7.5 cm (1–3 in), (second layer)

■ Silk fabric for chopped silk, strips 1.5 (⅝ in) wide

■ Embroidery threads and yarns such as stranded cotton, perle 8 or 12, silk and rayon in colours to match or contrast the fabrics (I used only stranded cottons here)

■ Ribbon, metallic gold 6 mm (¼ in) wide

■ Metallic gold twist thread for body and outline of butterfly and four circular motifs

■ 1 strand sewing silk or cotton, mustard yellow (DMC 783) for couching

■ Metallic thread, 3-ply, such as DMC fil d'or gold, 'Butterfly' gold, or Madeira 9805/5012 for chopped silk and all butterfly wings

**materials** continued over page >

*Detail of butterfly*

The extensively stitched background combined with the frayed edges of the silk becomes a rich designer textile to make into an object or article such as the front of a vest, clothing detail, bag, cushion or panel.

The butterfly's wings are stitched with chopped silk, using different colours for the upper and lower wings, beads and straight stitches in metallic thread, and outlined with metallic gold twist. Its body is decorated with bugle beads and the head is a gold jug bead with two small round beads for eyes.

Below the butterfly five applied wing shapes are edged with herringbone stitch and decorated with circular motifs of metallic gold twist thread and bugle beads. To the left and right of the butterfly, two richly textured rectangular areas are created with metallic ribbon and cords overstitched with chopped silk, bullions and strings of beads.

The finished embroidery may be framed or attached to an article of clothing, a cushion or bag.

## method

Collage silk dupion, overlapping edges 1 cm (⅜ in) (second layer) onto muslin (first layer/lining), the same size as the finished size given, and tack into place. Attach pieces with small running stitches in 1 strand matching cotton 3 mm (⅛ in) in from the edges. Embroider only to within 5 mm (¼ in) of the outside edges of the collage.

From the diagram, transfer the five applied wing shapes, 1; the five ovals, 2; circular motifs, 3; outline of the butterfly, 4; antennae, 5; head, 6; and body, 7. Work the elements of the design in the following order.

### 1 overlapping wings

Cut out five wing shapes in silk and tack them to the background. Stitch around the shapes with random herringbone stitch using 1 strand cotton.

### 2 ovals

Run-stitch an oval on each wing with metallic thread, 3-ply.

### 3 circular motifs

Attach a group of nine bugle beads in the centre of three of the wings and couch a single length of metallic gold twist thread around and over them. Repeat this circular motif above the butterfly.

### background

Merge the background collage with patterns of running stitch and scattered straight stitches with bugle beads using 1 strand cotton. Work vertical straight stitches on some of the edges of the silk.

**materials** continued

■ Cord, twisted metallic 2–4 mm (¹⁄₁₆–³⁄₁₆ in) diameter for two rectangular areas of rich texture

■ Clear adhesive fabric or craft glue

■ Beads: bugle 4 mm (³⁄₁₆ in) (scattered on background, chopped silk, 4 circular motifs and two lower wings of butterfly); bugle 5 mm (¼ in) (two upper wings); large and medium round dress beads (two rich textured areas); 1 gold jug bead, approximately 4 mm (³⁄₁₆ in) diameter, and 2 medium round dress beads for the head and eyes; 7 bugle beads, 5 mm (¼ in) for butterfly body

■ Beading needle

■ Beading thread (or size 50 sewing cotton pulled through beeswax)

■ Sewing cotton or 1 strand embroidery cotton for tacking

■ Embroidery frame, 30.5 cm (12 in)

■ Pins

■ Needles: embroidery, assorted sizes 3 to 7 or larger as needed

## layout and stitch guide

 cord

 beads

 bullion

 metallic gold ribbon

 chopped silk

 straight stitches

 bugle beads

 random herringbone stitch, 1 strand

——— edge of fabric

- - - - edge of frayed fabric

— — running stitches

enlarge diagram
by 215%

### 4 butterfly

Fill the wings with chopped silk, bugle beads and cross stitches in metallic gold thread, 3-ply. Stitch over the wings with long diagonal straight stitches in the same thread.

Couch two lengths of gold twist together around the outlines of the wings and the body (see detail).

**5 antennae** Couch one length of gold twist on each of the antennae.

**6 head** Attach the jug bead and two medium round dress beads for the head.

Variations of wrapping and beading are made over two rows of blanket stitch worked back-to-back. The stepped base of the collage is decorated with a fringe of beaded pendants to add an exotic touch.

## method

Collage silk dupion, overlapping edges 1 cm (⅜ in) (second layer) onto muslin lining (first layer), the same size as the finished size given, and tack into place. Attach them with small running stitches in 1 strand matching cotton 3 mm (⅛ in) in from the edges. Embroider only to within 5 mm (¼ in) of the outside edges of the collage.

From the diagram, transfer the outlines of the hand, A, and peacock, C, onto the fabric. Stitch two pieces of metallic ribbon, D, and a length of metallic cord, P, into place. Work wrapped blanket stitch, chopped silk, beading and other stitches using the photo and diagram as guides.

**A** Outlines of hand and peacock: couched gold twist and imitation Japanese gold.

**B** Peacock, crown, beak, feet and tail: straight stitches, 3 strands cotton and added beads at crown and tail.

**C** Peacock, body–feature bead, C1, bugle and medium round beads.

**D** Metallic ribbon.

## blanket stitch, E–P:

Two rows of blanket stitch are worked back-to-back and wrapped with different threads or beads as follows:

**E** Multiple wrapping in perle 5 cotton every second space to form 'thread beads'.

**F** Strings of small round beads.

**G** Metallic thread wrapped with loose, graduating to tight, tension.

**H** Flat round beads and small round beads.

**I** Metallic thread wrapped tightly.

**J** Bugle beads.

**materials** continued

■ Sewing silk or stranded cotton, mustard yellow (DMC 783) to attach cord, or pulled through beeswax to couch metallic thread

■ Clear adhesive fabric or craft glue

■ Metallic ribbon 1 cm (⅜ in) wide

■ Beads, such as bugle 5 mm (¼ in) long and large and medium round dress beads

■ Beading needle

■ Beading thread (or size 50 sewing cotton pulled through beeswax)

■ Sewing cotton or 1 strand embroidery cotton for tacking

■ Embroidery frame, 30.5 cm (12 in)

■ Needles: embroidery, assorted sizes 1 to 9 or larger as needed; tapestry, sizes 18 to 24 or larger as needed; milliners/straw, size 3

■ Pins

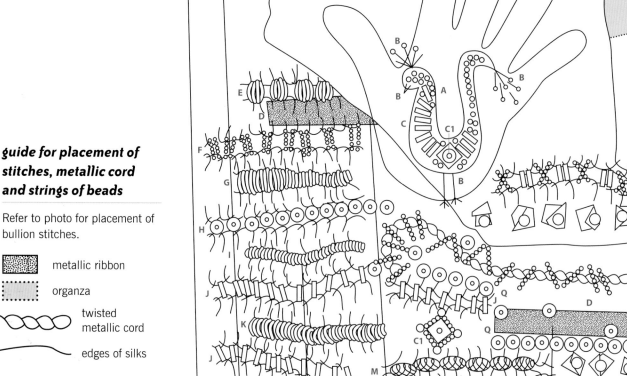

### guide for placement of stitches, metallic cord and strings of beads

Refer to photo for placement of bullion stitches.

 metallic ribbon

organza

 twisted metallic cord

edges of silks

| enlarge diagram by 135% |

**K** Multiple rows of thick twisted silk.

**L** Bugle beads and crossed strings of small round beads.

**M** Overlapping herringbone stitch, spaced to form 'beads', in metallic thread.

**N** Overlapping herringbone stitch in variegated perle 5 cotton.

**O** Chopped silk.

**P** Metallic cord overstitched with strings of beads alternating with bullion stitches.

Detail of Bird in the hand:

**P** *metallic cord overstitched with strings of small round beads*

**O** *chopped silk & beads*

**D** *metallic ribbon*

**Q** *flat round and small round beads*

**M** *overlapping herringbone stitch*

**N** *overlapping herringbone stitch in variegated perle 5*

## beading:

**Q** Apply flat round beads and small round beads individually and in rows.

To complete the work, attach a fringe of beaded pendants to the bottom edge of the fabric collage (see Section 7, Finishing and making up).

Cut off excess muslin and make up into a bag or a panel.

# concertina stitch book

A concertina cloth book like this is both a work of art and a wonderful way to present stitch samples and experiments for reference. You can begin with as few or as many pages as you like, and extra pages can be added at any time.

## materials

■ Interfacing: calico or homespun, approximately 80 x 60 cm (31 ½ x 23 ¾ in) for a 12-page book, cut into squares (see instructions)

■ Silk dupion, 24 pieces 16.2 cm (6 ⅜ in) square

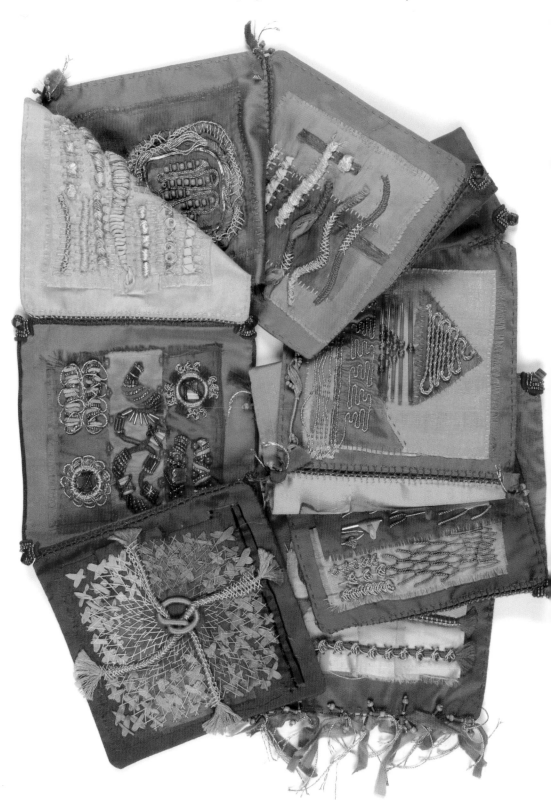

Each page is completed separately by the 'bagging' method, then joined with knotted buttonhole insertion stitch to the sides of other pages. The backs of the pages may be embroidered, collaged or left plain.

The option of making up the book pages on two layers of torn organza is also given. Alternatively, the pages may be joined together as a traditional book with a 'spine', using the same insertion stitch.

## method 1: making up the pages with calico backing

### step 1

On the calico or homespun draw twelve 15 cm (5 ⅞ in) squares (the finished size of the page) following the pattern diagram, with pencil and ruler, and then add seam allowance of 12 mm (½ in) all around.
See A in photo 1. Cut them out on the seam allowance line for a finished size of 16.2 cm (6 ⅜ in) square.
For each page, take 2 pieces of the silk dupion.
See B in photo 1.

### step 2

Take one piece of silk dupion and the interfacing, with the pattern outline facing up, and pin and tack them together with contrasting thread on the line indicating the size of the finished page. See C in photo 2.
Attach the collage with decorative or concealed stitches to the silk dupion, using the tacking line as a guide to position it in the centre.

### step 3

The front of the page is now ready to be attached to the back, the other piece of silk dupion. With right sides of silk dupion together, and interfacing showing the page size facing outwards, pin and tack the pieces together 3 mm (⅛ in) in from the page size (to allow machine stitching to be worked accurately along the pencilled line). Remove the previous tacking indicating the size of the finished page. Machine stitch front and back together on the finished page line, C in photo 2, except for a gap of 8 cm (3 ⅛ in) on one side, D–E in photo 2, preferably on one of the sides so that it will be concealed by the insertion stitch joining the pages together.

*pattern for book pages*

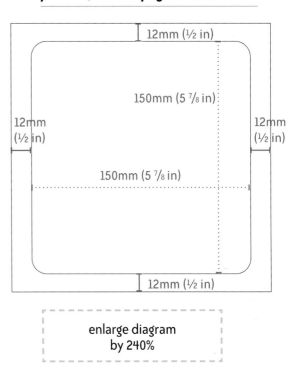

12mm (½ in)

150mm (5 ⅞ in)

12mm (½ in)    12mm (½ in)

150mm (5 ⅞ in)

12mm (½ in)

enlarge diagram by 240%

### photo 1

*Calico interfacing, A, and 2 layers of silk dupion, B, to make one page*

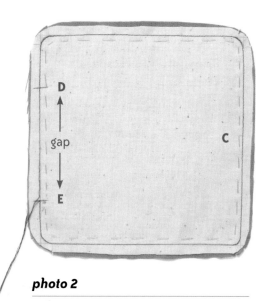

**photo 2**

*Machine stitching line, C, gap D–E*

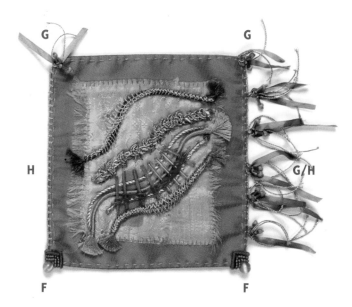

**photo 3**

*Finished page with trimmings of beads and bullion stitches on lower corners, F, silk strips and/or ribbons, metallic threads and beads on upper corners (and along the edge of the last page of the book), G, and knotted buttonhole insertion stitch on both sides, H.*

*A good tip for a smooth, straight finish to the edge of any article made using this bagging method is to start machine stitching at the beginning of the gap, D, with very long stitches until the end of the gap, E, then to use normal length stitches all around to the beginning. Finger-press the seam allowance over the machine stitching and unpick the long stitches across the gap before the next step.*

### step 4

Nick the seam allowance three times on each corner or trim the corners to approximately 2-3 mm ($\frac{1}{8}$ in).
See photo 2.
Turn the page out to the right side carefully, pushing the corners out by pulling them gently with a needle. Pin across the gap and close it with ladder stitch. Finger-press the edges of the page and tack them with sewing cotton.
Press the page on the back with an iron, front face-down on a folded bath towel. If necessary, spray a light mist of water onto the silk. Press the front and back edges flat on the ironing board without the towel.
Remove the tacking, press the page again and stitch a line of running stitch 3 mm ($\frac{1}{8}$ in) in from the edge with one strand of cotton. Photo 3 shows a finished page ready for joining.

### step 5

Before joining the pages, decide the order of the twelve pages and decorate some of the corners. The corners of every third page are left plain. These pages are separated by a page with corners decorated with beads and bullion stitch, F in photo 3, and a page with each corner decorated with one narrow torn or cut strip of silk habutai or silk ribbon and two lengths of metallic gold twist thread tied together in an overhand knot and attached with two beaded pendants, G in photo 3.

### step 6

Join the pages together with knotted buttonhole insertion stitch, H in photo 3.
Two sides of each page (except the 'outer' side of the first page) are stitched with knotted buttonhole insertion stitch, using perle 8 or 6 strands cotton spaced approximately 4 mm ($\frac{3}{16}$ in) apart, G in photo 3.

Two pages are joined at a time, held with right sides together while wrapping the loops of knotted buttonhole twice with the same thread, as shown in photo 3. The loops need not be wrapped strictly in alignment.

**step 7**
The 'outer' edge of the last page is stitched with knotted buttonhole insertion stitch, seven loops of which are tied with the same arrangements of strips of silk or ribbon, metallic gold twist thread and beaded pendants described above in step 5, H in photo 3.

**method 2: making up the pages with organza backing**
A very attractive option for making the pages for a concertina book is to attach the collage to two layers of torn organza and machine or hand-stitch the sides together, leaving a seam allowance of 2 cm (¾ in) and finished with raw edges all around. See photo 4.

**step 1**
Decide on the size of the page, for example, a finished size of 15 cm (5 ⅞ in) square, the same size as the concertina stitch book in Method 1. Add 2 cm (3/4 in) on both sides of the square, making a rectangle 19 cm (7 ½ in) wide by 15 cm (5 ⅞ in) and tear two rectangles of organza the same size.

**step 2**
Attach the collage to the two layers of organza. Cover the back with another collage or appliqué to conceal the back of the work from the front page.

Hand-stitch the sides of pages together with running stitch, leaving 2 cm (¾ in) seam allowance so that the finished page is 15 cm (5 ⅞ in) square.

*photo 4*

'Bilingual concertina stitch book', *with two layers of torn or cut organza used for the pages, shown with its book bag underneath and to the left.*

# coat for an angel

Closely worked detached chain stitches, one side wrapped, are ideal for interpreting the wings of this angel, inspired by a painting of an angel in a fresco in a church in Florence.

## finished size of panel approx 25 x 19 cm (9 ⅞ x 7 ½ in)

### materials

■ Indian muslin, 28 cm x 22 cm (11 x 8 ⅝ in): 1, 2 or more layers depending on the weight of the muslin and your preference; zigzag stitch or overlock the edges together before attaching to a frame (first layer/lining)

■ Silk dupion for the background (second layer)

■ Embroidery threads, stranded cotton or silk

■ Metallic thread equal to perle 8 in thickness, such as Madeira 9803/3008 for overlapping herringbone stitch on the arms

■ Metallic thread, 3-ply such as DMC fil d'or (gold) or 'Butterfly' gold for the halo

■ Metallic gold twist thread, imitation Japanese gold and 1 strand sewing silk or cotton in mustard yellow (DMC 783) pulled through beeswax for couching the coat outline

■ Clear adhesive fabric or craft glue

■ Beads, small round

■ Beading needle

■ Beading thread (or size 50 sewing cotton pulled through beeswax)

■ Cord, rat-tail or wrapped, for arms

■ Sewing cotton or 1 strand embroidery cotton for tacking

■ Embroidery frame, 30.5 cm (12 in)

■ Pins

■ Needles: embroidery, assorted sizes 3 to 7 or larger as needed

Triangles of space-dyed silk habutai applied with straight stitches on the gown make a smooth contrast to the textured surface of the wings, and the arms are interpreted in overlapping herringbone overstitching a wrapped cord.
The ringlets seen on Byzantine angels are suggested by soft buttonholed rings, and the halo is worked in several layers of herringbone stitch in metallic threads. Movement is created by running stitches on the background and swirls of metallic threads outlining the coat.

### method

Pin silk dupion (second layer) onto muslin (first layer/lining) and tack into place. Embroider only to within 5 mm (¼ in) of the outside edges of the fabric. Transfer the design from the diagram to the fabric.
Stitch this design guided by the diagram and photo.

**wings** Detached chains, one side wrapped, starting at the tips of the wings and working upwards. With 3 strands cotton or silk, work two detached chains on top of one another and wrap one side.

**gown** Triangles of space-dyed silk habutai applied with straight stitches.

**arms** Cord, wrapped or rat-tail, overstitched with overlapping herringbone stitch using metallic thread equal to perle 8 in thickness.

**neckpiece** Small round beads.

**halo** Two overlapping rows of herringbone stitch in fine metallic thread and one strand cotton, dotted with the same small round beads as the neckpiece.

**hair** Buttonholed rings made with three strands cotton around a skewer stick.

**eyebrows** Fly stitches in fine 3-ply metallic thread.

**eyes** Small stem stitches with one strand cotton.

**nose, mouth** Straight stitches in fine 3-ply metallic thread and one strand cotton.

**coat** Metallic gold twist and imitation Japanese gold threads couched in pairs, separating in places as shown on the diagram.

**background** One strand cotton or silk running stitch from the level of the arms.

Cut off excess muslin and make into a panel or other article.

*pattern and stitch guide*

enlarge diagram
by 170%

# cords
## for embellishment & trimming

Wrapped cord making evolved out of my experiences in learning to braid hair with stranded cotton. The next step translated the technique away from the hair, adding beads and experimenting. Continuous needle-wrapped cords evolved through a combination of hair braids and whipped stitches.

# wrapped & beaded cords

Wrapped and beaded cords are rich in contrasts of colour and texture, shiny and matt reflections, thick and thin core yarns. To further enrich the effect, overhand knots are tied in the cord and extra beads added. The ends can be finished with knots, loops or a beaded pendant tassel.
The cords are used singly, plaited, and/or twisted with other cords. Their many other applications include couching them to fabric to add pattern and texture, as handles and/or decorations for bags, as decorations for cushions and clothing, and as body adornments such as neckpieces, bracelets and amulets.

## ways of making cords include:

- Wrapping the whole cord without beads
- Leaving spaces unwrapped to reveal the core yarns without beads
- Including a string of beads and reveal them on top of exposed core yarn
- Including a string of beads and revealing them on top of wrapping
- Including a string of beads and wrapping it around the cord
- Attaching extra beads after wrapping.

*Pendant tassels and knotted cords. Striking cords are made by using vibrant and colourful beads and threads together with combinations of wrapped and beaded cords, knotted and beaded pendant tassels.*

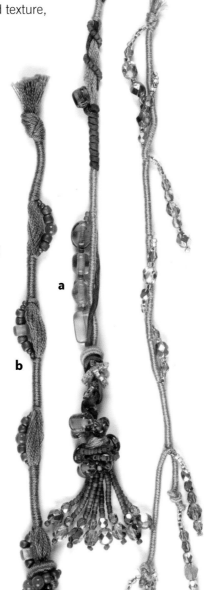

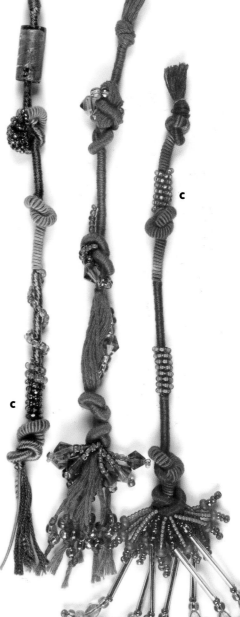

**a** *beads on top of wrapping*

**b** *beads with core thread revealed*

**c** *beads wrapped around the core*

## materials

- Beading thread (or size 50 sewing cotton pulled through beeswax)

- Beading needle or size 10 embroidery needle, depending on the size of the hole

- Beads, all kinds

- Threads for wrapping; start with stranded cottons, one or more colours

- Masking tape

- Cotton reel, pencil or small cylinder to wind bead string around the cord (optional)

## preparation

### Threads for core yarns and wrapping

Cut threads for core yarns and wrapping into 1–1.5 m (1–1 ½ yd) lengths: for thinner cord use 8 lengths, for medium cord 18 lengths, for thicker cord 30 or more lengths. The core yarns are also used for wrapping.

### Bead strings

Prepare a bead string by threading a beading needle with 1–2 m (1–3 yd) beading thread, double it and knot the ends together.

Gather core yarns and bead string (the knotted end) together and tie them with an overhand knot. The needle is left free at the other end to pick up beads as the wrapping progresses.

---

## tips for successful cord making

- *For ease of handling, work with 1 to 1.5 m (1–1 ½ yd) lengths of thread.*

- *Include additional lengths of the same size as needed to lengthen the cord.*

- *Use stranded cottons to start with—they are easy to wrap and produce a beautiful cord.*

- *Vary the number of lengths of thread in the core yarn to produce the desired thickness. For example, use approximately 8 lengths for a thinner cord, 18 for medium and 30 or more for thicker cords.*

- *Use beading thread or waxed size 50 sewing cotton to thread beads with smaller holes and 6 strands embroidery cotton in a matching colour for beads with larger holes.*

- *The left hand holds the core yarn at tension and facilitates the right hand, like a shuttle, while the right hand wraps.*

- *The right hand controls the wrapping thread by holding it at tension and feeding it to the left hand, which pulls it behind the core yarn and feeds it back to the right hand.*

- *Hold the wrapping thread in the right hand approximately 8 cm (3 ⅛ in) away from core yarn.*

- *The wrapping thread and core yarns must be held firmly while wrapping.*

- *Different colours may be used in the one cord. To change the colour of the wrapping thread, exchange one yarn with another at any point without a half-hitch knot.*

- *The effect is more dramatic when knots are tied over beaded areas of wrapped cord, and elegantly simple when knots are tied over lengths of plain wrapped cord. Knots use up quite a bit of wrapping and should be tied before finishing off the cord.*

- *To make a very stiff cord, as used in Project 6 'Butterflies out of a box' and Project 25 'Quattro bastoni', push the wrapping backwards from time to time to compress the coils.*

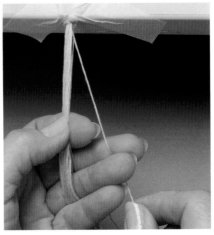

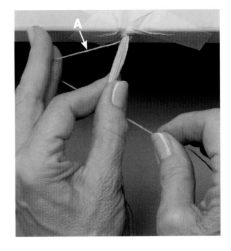

## method

**step 1** Attach the knotted end to a table or desk with masking tape. Separate 1 length (6 strands) and hold it firmly in the right hand.

**step 2** Hold the core yarns and bead string with firm tension between the thumb and forefinger of the left hand approximately 8 cm (3 ⅛ in) away from the wrapping point. Rotate the left hand until it is palm up and pick up the wrapping thread between the middle and ring fingers.

**step 3** Rotate the left hand until it is palm down. The right hand picks up the wrapping thread at A and …

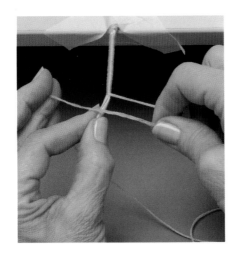

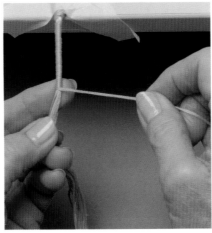

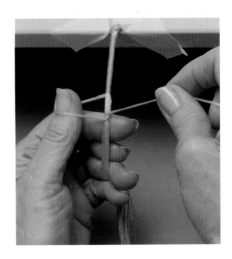

pulls it horizontally into position. Wrap with very firm tension. Right handers wrap clockwise, left handers anti-clockwise.

**step 4** Repeat above and continue wrapping or devise your own method. No gaps should appear between the wraps. Alternate the core yarns to use as wrapping thread.

**step 5** Pause and park to stop and secure wrapping thread to fasten off or prevent unravelling (or take a break). Tie the wrapping thread with a half-hitch knot.

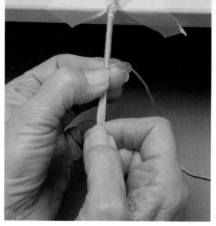

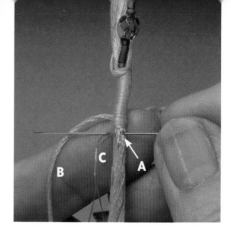

**step 6** If more wrapping threads are needed, add one or more 1–1.5 m (1-1 ½ yd) length/s of core yarn as needed by placing it/them under a half-hitch knot, A.
Continue wrapping to secure them and cut off the tail at A.

**step 7** Compress after wrapping for about 6 cm (2 ⅜ in) and parking the wrapping thread. To compress the wraps, hold the core at tension with the right hand while the left hand pushes the wrapping backwards. A length of 6 cm (2 ⅜ in) compresses to approximately 3 cm (1 ³⁄₁₆ in) of stiff cord.

**step 8** Pick up beads with the needle as required. When the bead string runs out, make another and secure the knotted end into the core at A. Continue wrapping, B, to cover the ends of the bead string, C.

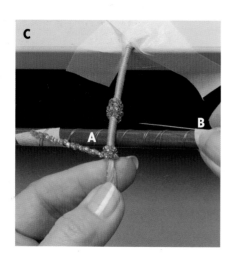

**step 9**

**a** Beads on top of wrapping are made by first separating the bead string from the core, wrapping around the core threads for the required distance and tying a half-hitch knot.
Add beads to the bead string and bring the bead string back into the core, tying a half-hitch knot around all of them with the wrapping thread. Continue wrapping with the bead string included in the core.

**b** Beads with core thread revealed. Add required beads, tie a half-hitch knot under the last bead and continue wrapping.

**c** Beads wrapped around core. Add required beads, push them together holding them taut, and wrap the bead string clockwise around core yarns as they are twisted anti-clockwise. Another method is to wrap the bead string around a cotton reel, pencil or small cylinder, A, securing it in place with masking tape, B. Hold the core yarn in the left hand while carefully wrapping the beads around it. Stitch the beading thread several times into the core and tie two half-hitch knots over it with wrapping thread.

*9a beads on top of wrapping*

*9b beads with core thread revealed*

*9c beads wrapped around the core*

*For full cords with tassels, see page 87.*

## finishing off: button and loop

**a Secure** cord at the beginning and cut off the knot.

**b Button:** secure cord as in a above, tie one or more knots and stitch them together with one strand of matching cotton.

**c Loop:** Ensure that a long wrapping thread is available to complete the loop. When the desired length of cord has been wrapped, continue plain wrapping for approximately 8 cm (3 ⅛ in), tapering the thickness of the core gradually by cutting off core yarns, and tie a half-hitch knot. Make a loop, test that it is the correct size for the knot and then wrap the end of the loop and cord together, A. Thread the end of the wrapping thread into a needle and take it back through the wrapping to finish. If necessary make the loop slightly larger and adjust to the correct size by stitching it with one strand of the same thread.

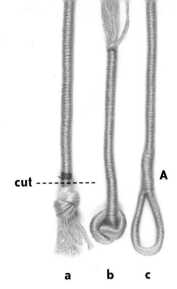

cut ----------

A

a     b     c

## finishing off: beads and knots

**Beaded pendant tassel:** Either secure and cut off the ends of the core and tie one or more knots, or leave the core to become part of the tassel. Attach beaded pendants and decorate the knot with beads.

**Wrapped** Before finishing off the cord, tie overhand knots to create texture.

### wrapped and beaded cords

*1 Core and wrapping stranded cotton and embroidery ribbon, overhand knots, 'Greek gold rings' sewn onto cord. Tassel of medium red beads alternating with gold rings, bugle and small round beads.*
*2 Core and wrapping stranded cotton and gimp cord, overhand knots, bead strings and gimp wrapped around core, large beads, wrapped and knotted tassel.*
*3 Core and wrapping stranded cotton, bead strings wrapped around core, small medium and large round beads, knotted beaded pendant tassel.*
*4 Neckpiece, knotted wrapping, flat square beads, pendant tassel.*
*5 Core and wrapping stranded cotton and fine, silk rouleaux, bullion stitches worked vertically over padding of wrapped thread, small beads and bullion stitches worked on top of an overhand knot with beaded pendants, round glass bead with hole.*
*6 Core and wrapping stranded cotton and embroidery ribbon, large round and assorted beads, wrapped and knotted tassel.*
*7 Core and wrapping stranded cotton, assorted coral and round beads, pendant tassel, three overhand knots on top of each other have created an exotic decorative knot for the tassel head.*

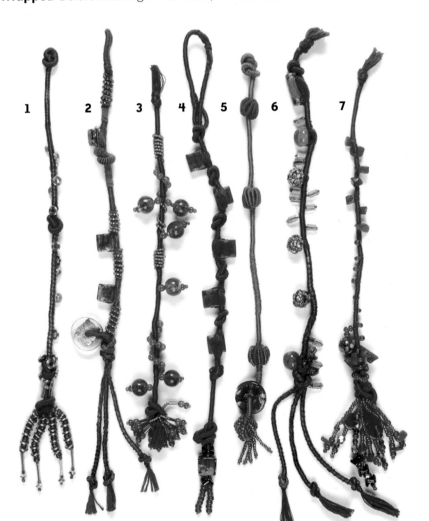

1    2    3    4    5    6    7

# aquamarine wrapped and beaded neckpiece

The wrapped and beaded cords technique is used to make this beaded neckpiece from beautiful knitting cotton, designed to be wound three times around the neck.

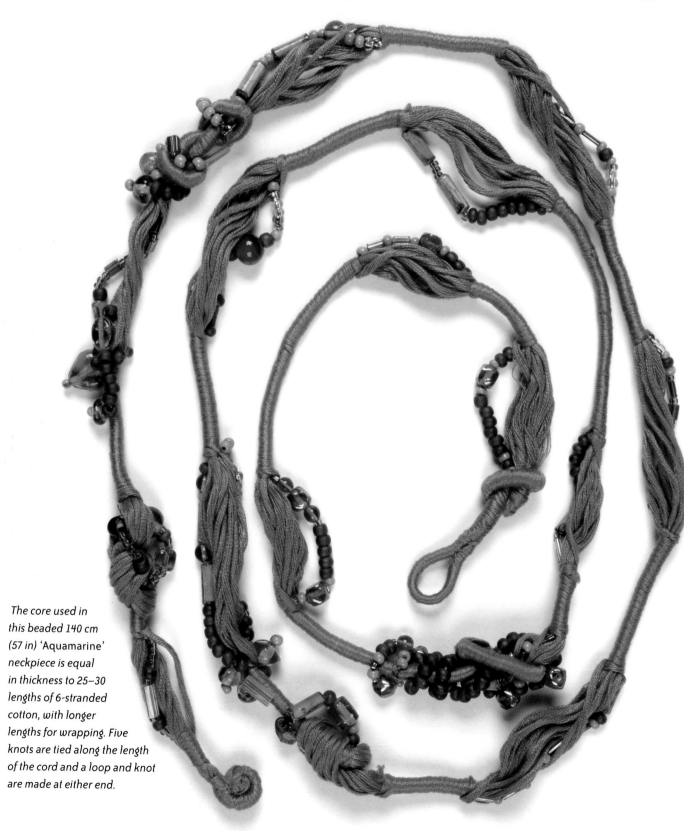

*The core used in this beaded 140 cm (57 in) 'Aquamarine' neckpiece is equal in thickness to 25–30 lengths of 6-stranded cotton, with longer lengths for wrapping. Five knots are tied along the length of the cord and a loop and knot are made at either end.*

# continuous cords made from needle wrapped threads

Continuous cords, made by wrapping tightly around a core of threads or yarns with a needle and thread, create unique three-dimensional textural relief. The cords may be thin or thick and are used to fill spaces, create lines, outlines, patterns, knots and spirals. Two or three cords may be knotted, plaited or twisted together.

I discovered this method while experimenting with hair braids, and with whipped stem and whipped back stitches in Casalguidi linen embroidery.

### the advantages of the continuous cord method are:

• The cords may be placed in designs where a ready-made cord has untidy ends, is unwieldy or too thick to make sharp corners and points.

• The cords begin and end at the back of the fabric and there is no need to finish the ends off like cords purchased by the meter (yard) or wrapped cords.

• A large range of colours is available when stranded cottons and other yarns are used.

• The thickness of the cord is easily varied to suit the desired size and scale by changing the number of strands used for the core and wrapping yarns. The three basic thicknesses are thick, made with a core of 2 lengths of 6 strands, wrapping 1 length of 6 strands; medium, made with a core of 1 length of 6 strands, wrapping 1 length of 6 strands; and thin, made with a core of 1 length of 6 strands, wrapping 1 length of 3 strands.

• Thicker cords may be made with more lengths in the core yarn but generally only one length of yarn or 6 strands cotton is used for the wrapping thread.

• The cord is made by attaching core yarns and a wrapping thread to the fabric. The wrapping thread is threaded in a needle for wrapping.

• A very strong, smooth, stiff cord is achieved when coils of wrapping are compressed periodically by pushing them back up the core.

**materials**

■ Fabric and threads: stranded cottons are recommended to start with

■ Tapestry needle size 24

■ Embroidery hoop or frame

*This is a detail from 'Nature strip', which appears in the Gallery toward the end of this book. See Project 22 'Waves and diamonds' and Project 23 'Sinuous shapes' for other examples of the use of continuous cords*

# continuous cords method instructions

Instructions shown are given for right-handers (left-handers reverse) using wrapping thread of approximately 1 m (1 yd) length of 6-stranded cotton in a size 24 tapestry needle wrapped around a core of two 50 cm (½ yd) lengths of 6 strands cotton as described above.

The thickness of both wrapping thread and core yarns may be varied for a thicker or thinner cord. Work in a frame or hoop, and for extra support clamp the hoop or frame to a table or pin fabric in a hoop to an ironing board.

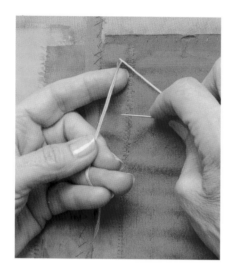

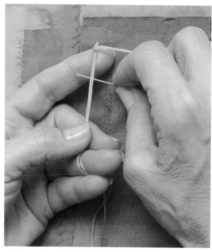

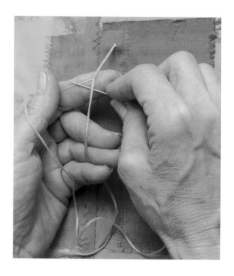

**step 1** Attach two 50 cm (½ yd) lengths of cotton (12 strands)—the core—and one 1m (1 yd) length cotton (6 strands)—the wrapping thread—to the back of the fabric in the frame or hoop and bring them to the front with a size 24 tapestry needle. Hold core yarns very firmly between the thumb and middle finger of the left hand, palm up, with the forefinger always under the core yarn at the wrapping point to prevent unravelling. The right hand wraps and maintains firm tension of the wrapping thread.

**step 2** Wrap clockwise, with right hand taking the needle and thread behind the core and bringing it out through the space made between the forefinger, middle finger and thumb. Pull tension very tightly with wraps next to each other.

**step 3** Pause and park. To pause wrapping, make a half-hitch knot (buttonhole stitch) around the core to 'park' it. Before commencing wrapping again, undo the knot with the needle while holding the core in the wrapping position as in step 2.

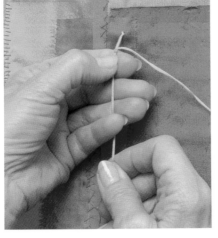

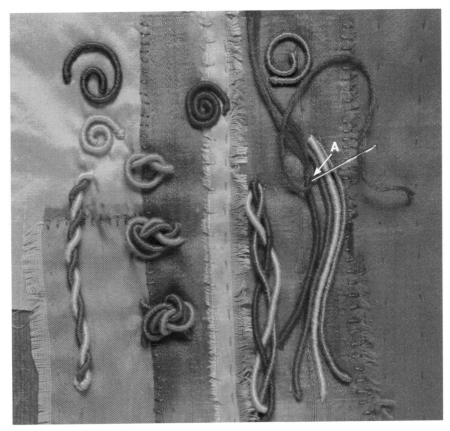

**step 4** Compress after wrapping for about 6 cm (2 ⅜ in) and parking the wrapping thread. To compress the wraps hold the core at tension with the right hand while the left hand pushes the wrapping backwards; a length of 6 cm (2 ⅜ in) compresses to approximately 3 cm (1 ³⁄₁₆ in) of stiff cord.

**step 5** Continuous cord may be made into spirals, lines, plaits, twists and knots. If the wrapping thread runs out midstream, pause and attach the cord to the design line with 1 strand thread of the same colour, coming out on the design line, around the cord and back into the same hole. Leave the core yarn at the front.
Start a new wrapping thread through the back of the work and bring the needle out through the exact point where the next wrap is to be made. When the cord is complete and sewn into place, take all the ends to the back one at a time with a needle and finish them off, A.

# waves & diamonds continuous cords

The versatility and beauty of continuous cords is demonstrated in this project where smooth, colourful cords are attached to the background fabric in wavy and overlapping lines and tied into one large and six smaller overhand knots to create rhythm and movement.

**finished size of collage (front of bag) 25 x 20 cm (9 ⁷⁄₈ x 8 in)**

## materials

Create your own palette of colours.

■ I used the following DMC colours in stranded cotton and perle:

- Wavy cords: C, stranded cotton 333 blue-violet; D, 552 violet; E, 601 pink; F, 721 apricot; G, 722 apricot light; H, 718 magenta
- Diamonds: stranded cotton in 721 apricot, 718 magenta, 3820 yellow
- Running stitches and appliqué: perle 8 in 783 yellow, 347 pink medium, 309 pink light
- Wrapped crosses: stranded cotton in 718 magenta, 917 magenta medium

■ Muslin for backing, 30 x 27 cm (11 ¾ x 10 ⁵⁄₈ in): 1, 2 or more layers depending on the weight of the muslin and your preference; zigzag stitch or overlock the edges together before attaching to a frame (first layer/lining)

■ Silk dupion and/or other rich fabrics for collage (second layer)

■ Embroidery threads: stranded cottons for continuous wrapped cords and perle 8 or other threads for running stitches

■ Embroidery frame, 30.5 cm (12 in)

■ Needles: embroidery, assorted sizes 1 to 9 or larger as needed; tapestry, 18 to 24 or larger as needed

■ Pins

A wealth of unique textures for three-dimensional effects is made by outlines and loops made of continuous cords to interpret diamond and other shapes. A patterned fabric of diamonds is the starting point for a background collage of warm, sunny colours covered with straight and spiral patterns of running stitches.

Running stitch patterns such as spirals may be worked straight onto the

The colour and threads used in this project are supplied as a guide. The finished collage is applied to another fabric and made into a page for a concertina stitch book shown in Project 19.

## method

Collage silk dupion, overlapping edges 1 cm (⅜ in), and organza (second layer) in a harmonious colour range onto muslin (first layer/lining), the same size as the finished size given, and tack into place. Attach the pieces with small running stitches in 1 strand matching cotton 3 mm (⅛ in) in from the edges. Embroider only to within 5 mm (¼ in) of the outside edges of the collage. Transfer the design by tacking the outlines shown on the diagram onto the fabric. Following the stitch guide, work the sinuous shapes.

**outer lines** A single metallic gold twist thread is couched with one strand silk or cotton in a matching colour.

**continuous cords for centre line of each shape** Start at the end of each shape at A, wrap the cord until there is enough to fold it at the top of each shape at B and finish approximately 1–1.5 cm (⅜–⅝ in) before the beginning. I used DMC violet 552 for the shape on the right, 553 for the shape on the left and 209 for the top shape. The core yarn of the cords is made from 12 strands plus wrapping yarn of 6 strands cotton. Stitch them in place adjacent to each other with one strand of cotton in the same colour.

Wavy couching over continuous wrapping Metallic thread was used for the wavy lines in all of the shapes and couched with two strands of cotton in the same colours as the continuous cords.

Starting at the top of each shape at B, attach the ends of the metallic thread at the back and bring it out to the front at B for couching with two strands cotton in the same colour as the continuous cords in an embroidery needle.

**shapes at top and right** From the diagram and photo, note the direction of couching. The couching stitches on the right hand shape are perpendicular to the continuous cord, while the couching stitches on the top are parallel to the continuous cord.

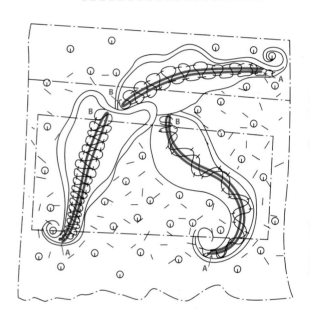

enlarge diagram by 160–165%

### layout and stitch guide

| | |
|---|---|
| ⊙ | sequins |
| —— · —— | edges of silk fabrics |
| ╱ ╲ ╱ ╱ | straight stitches |
| ⌇ | continuous cord |

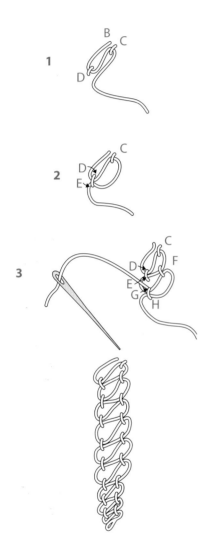

**shape on the left** Here the repeating pattern of loops resembles a diagonal figure-of-eight, and all the couching stitches are made parallel to the continuous cord. See diagram.

*Step 1* Bring the metallic thread out at B and make a loop. Couch a small stitch with two strands cotton at C first then at D

*Step 2* Loop the metallic thread around and under D and make another couching stitch from and on top of D to E

*Step 3* Loop the metallic thread around to F and make another small stitch. Adjust the loop to the correct size and bring the needle out at G to make a couching stitch below E. Adjust the loop and make another couching stitch from G to H.

*Step 4* Repeat to end of shape.

Following the stitch guide, work the background, embroidering scattered straight stitches and applying the sequins with one strand of space-dyed cotton or silk. Cut off excess muslin and make the embroidered collage into a book page for Project 19.

*Steps in wavy couching for on the left*

# red & gold cords, stitches and beads (book page)

All types of cords and buttonholed rings may be decorated.

**finished size for book page collage approx 11.5 to 12 cm (4 ½ to 4 ¾ in) square**

**materials**

Create your own palette of colours.

■ Indian muslin, 25 cm (9 ⅞ in) square: 1, 2 or more layers depending on the weight of the muslin and your preference; zigzag stitch or overlock the edges together before attaching to a frame (first layer/lining)

■ Silk dupion for the background (second layer)

■ Embroidery threads: stranded silk and cotton, perle 5 cotton for the bars of raised chain band

■ Metallic thread equal to perle 8 such as Madeira 9803/3007 or 3008 for wavy couching and buttonholed rings and 1 strand sewing silk or cotton pulled through beeswax, DMC 783 mustard yellow, for couching

■ Metallic gold twist thread for multiples of raised chain band

■ Cord, twisted metallic 6 mm (1/4 in) diameter to be covered with bullion stitches, bead strings and wavy couching on top right and lower left panels

■ Clear adhesive fabric or craft glue

■ Cord, rat tail or other as shown in middle panel

■ Rings, plastic or non-rusting metal, approximately 2 cm (¾ in) in diameter for buttonholed rings in top left and lower right panels

materials continued over page >

In this project I have used stitches such as raised chain band, cross, straight, bullions and wavy couching as well as bugle beads and strings of round beads, worked on a collage of silk which is then applied to another fabric and made into a page for the concertina stitch book in Project 19.

## method

Collage the silk dupion, (see photo), overlapping edges 1 cm (⅜ in) (second layer) onto muslin (first layer/lining), the same size as the finished size given, and tack into place. Attach the pieces with small running stitches in 1 strand matching cotton 3 mm (⅛ in) in from the edges. Embroider only to within 5 mm (¼ in) of the outside edges of the collage.

## upper panel

*Left side* Cover a metal or plastic ring with buttonhole stitch using metallic thread, and attach it to the fabric with the remaining tail of thread. Couch

**materials** continued

■ Beads, bugle, and small and medium round

■ Beading needle

■ Beading thread (or size 50 sewing cotton pulled through beeswax)

■ Sewing cotton or 1 strand embroidery cotton for tacking

■ Embroidery frame, 30.5 cm (12 in), or

■ Embroidery hoop 15–18 cm (6 in 7 in)

■ Pins

■ Needles: embroidery, assorted sizes 3 to 7 or larger as needed

*Red and gold': three panels of applied cords and buttonholed rings*

metallic twist thread or other thread around the ring, and stitch wavy couching on top of the ring and the couched metallic thread, guided by the photo. In the centre add bullion beads 'captured' with a cross of two strings of small beads. *Right side* Cut and secure the ends of two lengths of twisted metallic cord and attach them to the fabric. Overstitch the cords with bullion stitches and bead strings and couch metallic thread in wavy lines over the top.

**middle panel**
Couch a length of cord to the fabric and overstitch it with bullion stitches, bead strings and groups of bugle beads 'captured' with crosses made by two strings of small beads, a cross and two straight stitches made with metallic thread over them.

**lower panel**
*Left side* Same as the right side of the upper panel.
*Right side* Cover a metal or plastic ring with buttonhole stitch using metallic thread and attach it to the fabric with the remaining tail of thread. In the centre add bullion beads 'captured' with a cross made by two strings of small beads. Attach bugle beads to the ring and the fabric as shown in the photo and work multiples of raised chain band in metallic gold twist thread on bars made with perle 5 cotton.

Cut off excess muslin and make the embroidered collage into a book page for Project 19.

# quattro bastoni
## overstitched wrapped cords (book page)

Four red cords overstitched in metallic threads create a rich
contrast of colour and texture on a collage of vibrant yellow silks

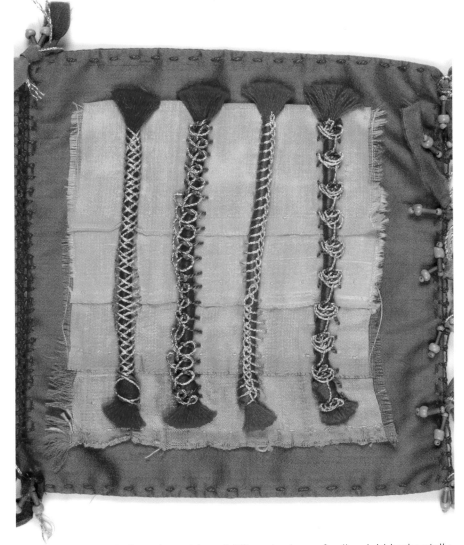

finished size for book page
collage approx 11.5 cm to 12
cm (4 ½ to 4 ¾ in) square.

### materials
Create your own palette of colours.

■ Indian muslin, 25 cm (9 ⅞ in)
square: 1, 2 or more layers depending
on the weight of the muslin and your
preference; zigzag stitch or overlock the
edges together before attaching to a
frame (first layer/lining)

■ Silk dupion and organza scraps and
strips for the background (second layer)

■ Embroidery threads: stranded cotton
for the wrapped cords; I used DMC
stranded cotton in reds 498, 321, 666
and 349 (approximately 1 skein per
colour) for the cords

■ Perle 5 cotton for the bars of raised
chain band

■ Metallic thread equal to perle 8 in
thickness such as Madeira 9803/3008

■ Metallic gold twist thread

■ Clear adhesive fabric or craft glue

■ Sewing cotton or 1  strand
embroidery cotton for tacking

■ Embroidery frame 30.5 cm, (12 in), or

■ Embroidery hoop, 15–18 cm (6–7 in)

■ Pins

■ Needles: Embroidery, assorted sizes
3 to 7 or larger as needed; tapestry,
sizes 16–24 or larger as needed

The collage is made from four strips of different values of yellow laid horizontally
and revealing their beautiful selvedges. The frayed edges of the ends of the
strips reveal the colours of the warp of the fabrics, which are sometimes
different from the colours of the weft. Where different colours are woven together
in a fabric, a more subtle or contrasting intermediate colour is produced.
Wrapped cords with knotted and tasselled ends have been used here rather
than bought cords, because of the wider colour range of colours available in the
stranded cottons used to make them. Stitches such as overlapping herringbone
stitch, raised chain band, Vandyke and multiples of raised chain band worked
over the cords produce an exciting three-dimensional surface.
The finished collage is applied to another fabric and made into a page for the
concertina stitch book shown in Project 19.

*Detail of a compressed wrapped
cord overstitched with:
left, Vandyke stitch;
right, raised chain band multiples.*

### method

Collage the silk dupion strips, overlapping edges 1 cm (⅜ in) (second layer) in a harmonious colour range onto muslin (first layer/lining), the same size as the finished size given. Attach the strips with small stitches in 1 strand matching cotton 3 mm (⅛ in) in from the edges. Embroider only to within 5 mm (¼ in) of the outside edges of the collage.

### wrapped cords

Make four wrapped cords from stranded cotton, finished length 11 cm (4 ⁵⁄₁₆ in) including tassels. The cores for each of the cords are made from 15 x 25 cm (10 in) lengths of 6 strands cotton, wrapped with an extra length of 6 strands cotton 2.2 m (2 ½ yd) long in reds, left to right, 498, 321, 666 and 349. These cords have been compressed while wrapping for a stiff cord.

### overstitching
### Left to right:

*Cord 1* Use metallic thread equal to perle 8 to overstitch overlapping herringbone stitch.
*Cord 2* Use metallic gold twist thread to overstitch raised chain band on bars made with perle 5.
*Cord 3* Use metallic thread equal to perle 8 to overstitch Vandyke stitch.
*Cord 4* Use metallic thread equal to perle 8 to overstitch raised chain band multiples on bars made with perle 5.

Cut off excess muslin and make the embroidered collage into a book page for Project 19.

# variations

## overlapping herringbone stitch (book page) A book page featuring lines and spots of overlapping herringbone stitch variations

I have always been fascinated with overlapping herringbone stitch after finding it many years ago in a book by Louisa F. Pesel titled Stitches from Eastern Embroideries, published around 1913. The stitch originated in Portugal, Crete and Hispano-Moresque Andalusia (medieval Spain) and is shown worked straight onto the fabric or padded with a cord.

My experiments have resulted in some variations which are explored in this book page and in Project 17 'Lime' and Project 18 'Bird in the hand'. They are called overlapping herringbone over thick cord or thread padding and overstitching with metallic threads.

A further variation is to use the pattern of the stitch to wrap two rows of blanket stitch worked back to back, where different weights of threads, embroidery ribbon, fine silk rouleaux, gimp, metallic threads, beads and sequins are used. I have called these variations overlapping herringbone over 2 rows blanket stitch, and overlapping herringbone, spaced, over 2 rows blanket stitch.

**finished size for book page collage approx 11.5 to 12 cm (4 ½ to 4 ¾ in) square**

### materials
Create your own palette of colours.

■ Indian muslin, 25 cm (9 ⅞ in) square: 1, 2 or more layers depending on the weight of the muslin and your preference; zigzag stitch or overlock the edges together before attaching to a frame (first layer/lining)

■ Silk dupion and/or silk habutai and organza strips or selvedge edges for the background (second layer)

■ Embroidery threads: stranded cotton or silk, cotton or silk equal to perle 5 and 8

■ Ribbon, silk embroidery 4 mm (³⁄₁₆ in)

■ Thread padding: stranded cotton or other yarns

■ Cord for padding

Metallic thread equal to perle 8 in thickness such as Madeira 9803/3008 for overstitching

■ Metallic gold twist thread

■ Clear adhesive fabric or craft glue

■ Sewing cotton or 1 strand embroidery cotton for tacking

■ Embroidery frame 30.5 cm (12 in) or

■ Embroidery hoop 15–18 cm (6–7 in)

■ Pins

■ Needles: embroidery, assorted sizes 3 to 7 or larger as needed; tapestry, assorted sizes or larger as needed

## materials continued

- Beads, bugle and small round

- Beading needle

- Beading thread (or size 50 sewing cotton pulled through beeswax)

- Sewing cotton or 1 strand embroidery cotton for tacking

- Embroidery frame, 30.5 cm (12 in), or

- Embroidery hoop, 15–18 cm (6–7 in)

- Pins

- Needles: embroidery, assorted sizes 3 to 7 or larger as needed; tapestry, assorted sizes

## thread padding Step-by-step guide to thread padding

(For more examples of thread padding and overstitching refer to Project 26 'Variations'.)

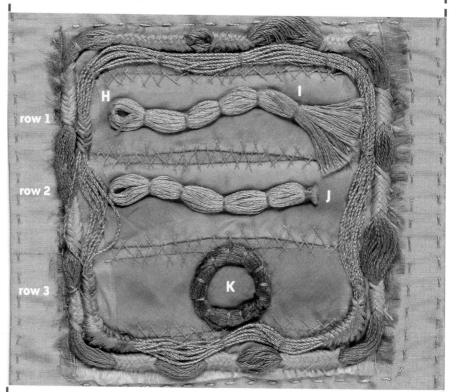

**row 1** *(step 1)* Cut 10 lengths of thread twice the length of the design line plus 8 cm (3 in) (for handling). Fold the bundle in half and make two stitches with sewing cotton to attach the loop to the design line, H. Make further stitches as loops coming out of the fabric, around the padding and back into the same hole, approximately every 2 cm (¾ in) to the end of the design line, I. These loops allow the padding to be cylindrical rather than flat (as with couching stitches). These looped stitches are temporary and are removed after overstitching.

**row 2** *(step 2)* Secure the ends of the padding threads with 8–10 stitches through and around them with sewing cotton and cut off excess, J.

**row 3** A circular shape can be made when the secured ends meet with the looped beginning, K.

An alternative way finishing off the tail ends of thread padding in a circular shape is to bypass step 2 above and take them to the back of the work one at a time with a needle.

## method

Collage the silk fabrics, overlapping edges 1 cm (⅜ in (second layer) onto muslin (first layer/lining), the same size as the finished size given, and tack into place. Attach the pieces with small running stitches in 1 strand matching cotton 3 mm (⅛ in) in from the edges. Embroider only to within 5 mm (¼ in) of the outside edges of the collage.
Transfer the design lines to the fabric.

## beaded collage centre

Apply a piece of silk fabric to the background with running stitches.
Following the stitch guide, couch a wavy line D-E of two strands of metallic copper twist thread, using herringbone stitch in 1 strand cotton or silk. Add alternating small bugle and medium beads in the spaces, F.

## inner border C

Following the layout and design diagram, couch two strands of imitation Japanese gold, G, or other metallic thread along the line C.

## middle border A

This border is made with two layers of stitching.
*First layer* Following the method outlined in the step-by-step guide, attach thread padding made from 10 lengths of metallic gold twist thread twice the length of the border plus 8 cm (3 in), folded in half, L.
*Second layer* Overstitch small areas of thread padding with tightly worked overlapping herringbone stitch with 6 strands silk or cotton.

## outer border B

This border is made with three layers.
*First layer* Following the method outlined in the step-by-step guide, attach thread padding made from 10 lengths of stranded cotton twice the length of the border plus 8 cm (3 in), folded in half, N.
*Second layer* Overstitch small areas of thread padding with tightly worked overlapping herringbone stitch with 6 strands silk or cotton, O.
*Third layer* Overstitch the whole border with irregular Vandyke stitches in metallic thread, with one or two loops through previous Vandyke stitches, some overlapping the inner border, P.

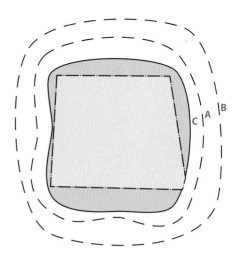

### layout and design lines for borders

| | |
|---|---|
| ▢ | silk fabric appliqué |
| ▨ | beaded collage centre |
| – – – | design lines for thread padding A and B |
| ——— | design lines for couched metallic threads, C |

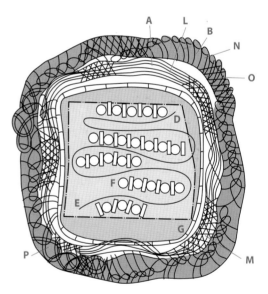

### stitch and thread padding guide

| | |
|---|---|
| ▢ | silk appliqué |
| ▨ | area of beaded collage |
| ≈ | **L** middle border A, metallic gold twist thread padding |
| ✕ | **M** middle border A, overlapping herringbone |
| ▦ | **N** outer border B, stranded cotton thread padding |
| ⊠ | **O** outer border B, overlapping herringbone |
| ⋈ | **P** Vandyke stitch |

# stitch & bead patterns

Stitches, beads, threads, ribbons and cords combine to create crunchy, touchy-feely textures

# mosaic bead & stitch patterns

Many thousands of years ago beads fashioned of bone, ivory and seeds fascinated the earliest human beings, progressing to embellishing clothing and to jewellery. Today beads are available in an infinite range of shapes and colours. They are beautiful, irresistible, touchable and exotic.

A unique surface is created in this project when beads are combined with silk, shiny metallic threads and cords, and blended and merged with embroidery. 'Touchy-feely', crunchy-textured surfaces and patterns are made with silk fabric and ribbons torn, cut and chopped, and combined with stitches, beads and metallic threads and cords. The colours of the threads you choose add to the impact of the beads because it shows at the sides of solid beads and through transparent beads.

Use the photo as a guide to creating your own combinations. Make up your work into a panel, bag or book page.

## method of attaching beads

Use a single strand of beading thread, not double. If you are using cotton thread pulled through beeswax, use one strand. Attach the thread securely to the back of the fabric and bring it to the front. Stitch twice through each bead or through a group of 2 or 3 beads.

Stitch twice through strings of beads over cords. Select the number of beads needed for the string of beads to be positioned over a cord. For odd lengths, that is, where the exact length measures 7 ½ beads for example, use one less bead (7), rather than one more (8), as an overlong string will not sit correctly.

## applying strings of beads

Applying strings of beads, as seen in the first panel in row 4, requires patience in controlling the level of the bead string and the tension of the stitches. Bring two needles to the front of the fabric, one with sewing cotton in a colour matching the beads in an embroidery needle to make stitches over the beading thread, and one with beading thread in a beading needle to hold the beads. Thread beads onto the beading thread and park the needle, adding or removing beads as needed to match the length being beaded. With the waxed cotton, make small stitches over the beading thread, between beads, following the curve and bringing the stitch out and going back down into the same hole with medium tension, to prevent 'dips' in the line of beads.

**finished size for each small square approx 6.3 cm (2 ½) square**

materials
- Beads
- Beading needles
- Beading thread (or size 50 sewing cottons pulled through beeswax)

*Opposite: Beads in silk bags*
*Below: Strings of beads in the first panel of row 4, 'Mosaic'*

### row 1

For a smooth surface to the fabric, without puckering, work this project on fabric laced and stretched in a frame.

*Left*: rows of running stitch in silk thread equal to perle 3, alternating with rows of bugle beads and round beads.

*Centre*: scattered bugle beads and straight stitches worked in 1, 2 and 3 strands of cotton.

*Right*: wave stitch in silk thread equal to perle 3, with twin broken lines of bugle beads suggesting running stitches; the beads in the third row are decorated with straight stitches in metallic thread.

### row 2

*Left*: threads of varying thickness couched with vertical straight stitches; bugle beads tied with straight and cross stitches in metallic thread, and medium size round dress beads.

*Centre*: lines of linked bullion stitch with an area of 'crunchy' mixed beads and rows of bugle beads and round beads. Some groups of three bugle beads are 'captured' with cross stitches in metallic thread.

*Right*: rows of detached chain wrapped together and decorated with bugle and small round beads. Some bugle beads in one row are captured with two or three straight stitches in metallic thread.

### row 3

*Left*: couched gold ribbon and cords, chopped silk with bugle beads and cross stitches in metallic threads, gold cords decorated with bullion stitches, bugle beads and strings of small round beads.

*Centre*: collage of torn silk, organza and ribbons stitched with detached chain half wrapped, bugle beads and various fancy beads.

*Right*: small squares of silk with edges lightly frayed, decorated with bugle beads, small round beads and some French knots.

### row 4

*Left*: couched cords and couched strings of small beads.

*Centre*: three sizes of couched metallic cords embellished with bullion stitches, bugle beads and strings of small and medium round dress beads.

*Right*: four groups of two rows of blanket stitch worked back to back are made with cotton, silk and metallic thread. The first row is wrapped with thick metallic thread, the second and fourth rows (metallic blanket stitch) are decorated with strings of small and medium round beads to imitate wrapping stitches, the third row with variegated silk thread equal to perle 3.

**Opposite**:
'Mosaic': silk over muslin beaded and stitched in twelve small squares, approximately 6.3cm (2 ½ in) each

# finishing & making up

Instructions for making up bags & cloth books, banners, beaded pendants
for tassels and fringes, as well as thread tassels & twisted cords

## bags and banners

### bags: bagged method

The front and back of a bag are made the same way as the front of a book page
(Project 19), except that the interfacing could be a padding such as thin quilt
wadding or pellon instead of calico. The front and back are joined together by
knotted buttonhole insertion or ladder stitch.

### bags and book pages mounted on organza

Collages for bags and book pages may be applied to two layers of cut or torn
organza instead of silk.

The front and back of a bag are each made from two layers of cut or torn
organza 1.5–2 cm (5/8–3/4 in) larger all around than the collage (a total of four
layers). The collage for the front is stitched onto two layers to make the front of
the bag, and the four layers are combined and joined together on the sides and
base with running stitches using one or two strands silk or cotton, 1.5–2 cm
(5/8–3/4 in) in from the edge. Use ready-made cord or make your own beaded
and wrapped cords for the handles.

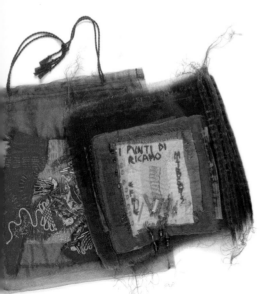

*Bilingual concertina stitch book
shown in Project 19.*

**book pages, concertina**
See Project 19.

**banners**
Banners are a lovely way to display and arrange collages and may be any size.
Finished collages are first applied to two layers of organza, 1.5 cm (⅝ in) larger
all around than the collage, and then stitched to the top layer of the banner.
The banner in the photo is made from one piece of silk and one piece of
organza on top, and measures 52 x 21 cm (20 ½ x 8 ¼ in); the side edges are
torn and slightly frayed. Enlarge or reduce this size to suit your purpose.
The tops of both fabrics are folded together to the back for 3 cm (1 3/16 in) and
run-stitched into place with two strands of cotton or silk to make a channel for
a wooden dowel stick 6 mm (¼ in) in diameter. The dowel stick is first wrapped
with a strip of organza 3 cm wide, with a little fabric glue applied at each end of
the stick to hold the organza in place. Fix small screw eyes into the ends of the
stick to hold fishing line or a cord for hanging the banner. Make a small hole first
using a fine nail and a hammer, then screw in the eyes.
Make a twisted cord or a wrapped and beaded cord to hang from the top, tying
each end of the cord through a screw eye with an overhand knot and adjusting
the length to suit your purpose.
The 'fringe' is twisted cords, each attached to the lower collage with a bead. The
twisted cords are made from two 50 cm (20 in) lengths of 6-stranded cotton
which results in cords approximately 16.5 cm (6 ½ in) long. Heavy beads are
attached to the bottom of the banner for decoration and to add weight to keep it
hanging straight.

# beaded pendants & fringes

Beaded pendants are attached to the ends of cords to make tassels or to the
edge of fabric or a bag to form a fringe, as seen in Project 18, 'Bird in the hand'.
Attach beading thread and needle very securely to the base fabric or cord to
start. Pick up an arrangement of beads onto the needle and thread, take it
around the last 'stopper' bead and back through all beads to the beginning.
Secure the thread with several stitches with the correct degree of tension, not
too tight, to allow the pendant to dangle smoothly.

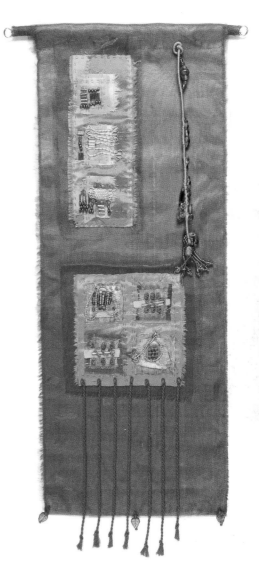

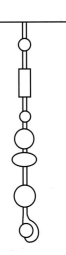

*Beaded pendant: direction of work*

# tassels & twisted cords

## twisted cords

The length of thread required to make a twisted cord is approximately four to six times the length of the finished cord. Multiply the number of lengths depending on the thickness of the cord. For example, 2 lengths of 6 strands cotton 2 m (2 yds) long results in a twisted cord approximately 75 cm (30 in) long.

**Step 1** Double the yarn around a hook or door handle and twist all the strands until tightly coiled.

**Step 2** Take the cut ends of the twisted yarn back to the hook or door handle, hold ends and twisted yarn firmly together with one hand, double the yarn and hold it taut with the index finger of the other hand at the midpoint. Rotate your index finger to start the cord twisting along its length, removing your finger before it gets trapped while still holding the two ends together with the other hand.

**Step 3** Let the cord twist back on itself, and knot the ends.

*Steps in making a twisted cord*

## tassels

These instructions are for a small tassel 3 cm (1 ¼ in) long made with perle 8 thread. Vary the measurements and threads to suit the scale of tassel you wish to make.

**Step 1** Cut a template of heavy card to the desired size, in this case 3 cm (1 ¼ in) square. Wind 80 wraps of perle 8 around the template, keeping the wraps narrower at the top, B, and fanning out at the bottom, A. Add the tying cord, 60 cm (24 in) of perle thread, doubled, in a tapestry needle, by inserting it between the wrapped thread and the card at the top or narrow end of the tassel, B. Remove the needle.

**Step 2** Tie two firm knots in the tying cord. Remove the tassel from the card. Tie the neck with 30.5 cm (12 in) of thread as follows: lay the thread on a table or your knee and place the tassel on top. Tie the neck, approximately 1 cm (⅜ in) once below the top, C, and turn the tassel over. Tie another two knots.

**Step 3** Wrap the remaining ends of the wrapping thread three times around the neck, then thread them into a tapestry needle and take them into the body of the tassel just above the neck and through into the skirt, D. Trim the ends. Cut and trim the skirt of the tassel.

*Steps in making a tassel*

desired number of times, pausing every 4–6 wraps to adjust the tension, stroking clockwise to tighten, anti-clockwise to loosen.

**4** Loosen the tension of the last 2 or 3 wraps slightly to prevent making a tight wrap at the top, which results in a pointed end to the bullion. Ensure that all wraps are even before pulling the thread through as uneven wraps result in uneven bullion stitches.

**5** Hold the wraps until all the thread is pulled through.

**6** Hold the end of the bullion stitch with a needle or your thumbnail while pulling the thread to the required tension.

**7** Finish into B for final tension.

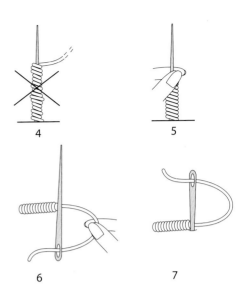

## bullion stitch, **long-armed**

This stitch is worked the same as regular bullion stitch between A and B to step 4. The finishing stitch is taken into the fabric a distance away at C.

## bullion stitch, **linked**

Bullion stitches are worked as above between A and B, being linked together with a long stitch, C-D, and repeated to make lines. The number of wraps may be varied and the space between rows depends on the thickness of thread.

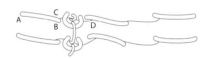

## bullion stitch, **linked and raised chain band**

Work rows of linked bullions in alignment, the spaces between the rows being dependent on the thickness of thread to be used for the raised chain band. Refer to detailed instructions for raised chain band below.

Work raised chain band on top of the links, bring the needle and thread out just above the centre of the link to be stitched.

row 1

row 3

row 4

row 7

*Lines of linked bullion are worked in rows with stitches in alignment as in row 1; random or alternating rows of bullion stitches underneath links as in rows 3 and 4; and raised chain band worked on the links as in row 7, Project 11 'Colour, texture and pattern'.*

## bullion stitch, patterns over cord

This detail shows bullion stitches worked over cord in Project 24, 'Red and gold'.
The technique is also used in Project 14 'Ancient eyes' and Project 18 'Bird in the hand'.

## buttonhole stitch rings, hard

Closely worked buttonhole stitches are made over metal or plastic rings to create the effect seen in Project 24 'Red and gold'. To begin attach the thread to the ring with a small amount of glue and work buttonhole stitch to cover it. Work a second layer of buttonhole stitches if necessary to cover any gaps between stitches.

## buttonhole stitch rings, soft

In this technique (see an example of buttonhole rings as ringlets of hair on the angel in Project 20 'Coat for an angel), buttonhole stitches are made around a pencil or couronne (ring) stick, even a wooden skewer stick, with thread. The tiny rings are stitched with 3 strands of cotton in a tapestry needle. Wind the end of the thread three or four times around the stick to create a core, anti-clockwise if working the buttonhole stitch from left to right, clockwise if stitching from right to left. Make closely worked buttonhole stitches with tight tension around the core, pulling the thread straight down level with the stick so that a ring, not a flat 'washer' shape, results. After a few of the buttonhole stitches are worked cut off the tail of the wrapping thread and continue stitching around the core to the first stitch. The last buttonhole stitch is taken into the loop of the first stitch from underneath. Use the tail to attach the ring to fabric, or finish off the thread by wrapping over three or four stitched loops and cut off excess thread.
If the thread runs out before finishing, bring in new thread following the tip for starting a new thread midstream.

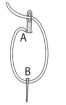

## chain stitch, detached

Make a single chain stitch by bringing the thread out at A, making a loop and taking the needle back into A and out at B. Tie the loop down into C.

## chain stitch, detached, wrapped on one side

An example of this stitch is seen in the angel's wings in Project 20 'Coat for an angel'. Refer to the tip wrapping stitches: tension control, above, for hints on wrapping. Make two chain stitches on top of each other with an embroidery needle and if necessary change to a tapestry needle for the wrapping. Bring the needle out at A, separate the sides of the chain stitch with the needle, wrap with firm tension halfway around to B, and finish the thread behind the last wrap. Place the wraps alongside each other. The second diagram shows the finished stitch.

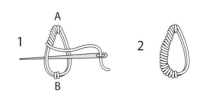

## chain stitch, detached, sides wrapped together

Work detached chain stitches side by side. Tie the outer sides of the endmost chains to help keep their open shape. Wrap one side of each of two chains together, starting at A, and finishing at B. Repeat for each pair of wrapped chains.

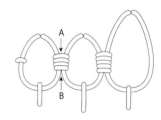

## chain stitch lines

Work a loop between A and B to start each new chain.

## chain stitch, two lines wrapped together

Work rows of chain stitches, spaced evenly or unevenly in wavy lines, close together for a solid linear effect, or spaced for a more lacy effect. Bring the needle out at A in the second row with wrapping thread, down at B through the loop directly above it and diagonally across to the next loop on the second row, A-B-C, ntf. A variation of this is to work more than one wrapping stitch around two chain loops

## chain stitch, lines whipped

Work a line of chain stitches starting at A and whip once over each chain, ntf.

## chain stitch, oyster variation

1  Make a twisted chain, A-B-C, pulling the thread at tension level with the fabric.
2  Stabilise the thread with the thumb and push the needle behind the cross, ntf.
3  Make a chain stitch around the twisted chain, inserting the needle into D above the cross and out at C again, and make a tying stitch into E which may be short or long. The tying stitch or any part of the chain stitches may be wrapped.

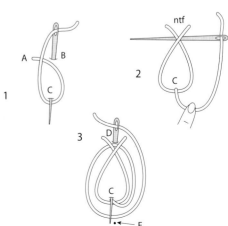

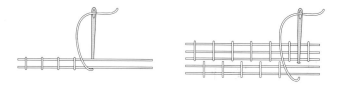

## couching

One or two lines of thread are couched together with straight stitches. When couching metallic threads use a strand of silk or cotton thread in a matching colour pulled through beeswax. When working more than one row lay the couching stitches in a brick pattern.

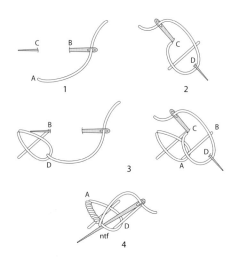
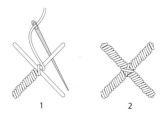

## cross stitch, chained, one side wrapped

This stitch may be used as a broad line or space filler. Each unit is worked on a square, A-B-C-D, and linked together by sharing D and B.

1  Make a half cross, A-B-C.
2  Insert needle in at C and out at D; loop thread around needle to make a chain stitch which completes the unit.
3  Repeat the above steps, sharing the holes made at B and D.
4  Wrap one side of the chain loop between A and D, using a tapestry needle and matching or contrasting thread.

## cross stitch, wrapped

1  Make a cross stitch, any size or angle desired, and wrap one arm of the cross, taking one wrap over the intersection.
2  Repeat on the other arm.
3  Combine with wrapped chains.

## fancy hem stitch

Two rows of stem or outline stitches are worked exactly opposite each other, then whipped together. A thread similar to perle 5 is recommended for the outline/stem stitch and any kind of matching thread can be used for the wrapping. Stitches may be worked as single units, lines or rows to fill shapes. Wrapping thread may be different from the foundation thread.

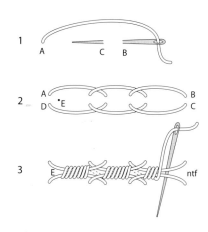

1  Outline stitch A-B-C. From A to B is approximately 1–1.5 cm (⅜–⅝ in); B-C is approximately 3 mm (⅛ in) long or about one-fifth of the length of A-B. Outline stitch is similar to stem stitch except the thread is held above the needle, not below, as it is worked.
2  Work two rows of outline stitches approximately 3 mm (⅛ in) apart, A-B and C-D, stitches opposite each other.
3  Bring needle out at E between the two rows to commence wrapping, working left to right. Wrap the two rows together using a tapestry needle, moving from one group to the next, ntf.

## f ly stitch and fly stitch, **wrapped**

Fly stitch is very versatile because of the many variations and arrangements that may be made with its three 'arms', one, two or all of which may be wrapped for extra texture.

**1** Fly stitch is made the same way as chain stitch, but is open at the top.

**2** Wrap all or parts of the stitch.

**3** Vary the shape by changing (a) the width, (b) the length of A-B-C, or (c) the length of C-D.

**4** Different arrangements of fly stitches, colour and threads evoke character to groups of fly stitches: (a) arranged geometrically they resemble tiles or mosaics; (b) randomly placed they resemble rocks, moss or forest, and (c) ferns, trees, wheat, grasses

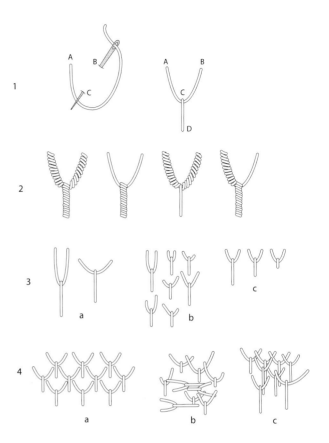

## french knot

**1** Bring needle out at A. Hold yarn with the thumb and first finger and rest the needle on top of the yarn.

**2** Wrap a loop towards you around the needle, B.

**3** Twist the needle sideways and towards you, C, and insert into the fabric a short distance away from A.

**4** Adjust the required tension and pull through, D.

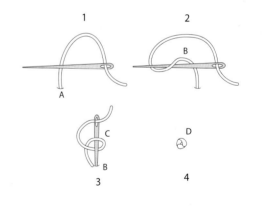

## herringbone stitch, **overlapping**

Vertical long crosses are worked in lines from the top down as shown in diagram, A-B-C-D. After working two crosses underneath each other to start, A-B-C-D and E-F-G-H, the subsequent crosses are positioned 2 stitches up on the right, across and out three stitches up on the left, I-J-K-L.

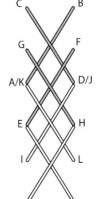

**herringbone stitch, overlapping, overstitched on cord**

'Quattro bastoni'; detail from cord on left.

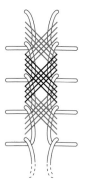

**herringbone stitch, overlapping, over 2 rows blanket stitch**

Overlapping herringbone is wrapped around two rows of blanket stitch worked back to back, ntf over each section, resulting in an uneven line. More than four crosses may be wrapped over each section of blanket stitches to create padded, raised 'thread beads'.

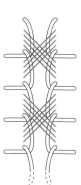

**herringbone stitch, overlapping, spaced, over 2 rows blanket stitch**

Overlapping herringbone is wrapped around two rows of blanket stitch worked back to back, ntf over every second section, leaving a space. More than four crosses may be wrapped over these to create padded, raised, 'thread beads'.

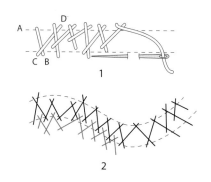

**herringbone stitch, random**

Herringbone stitch consists of straight stitches, A-B-C-D, that are crossed to form a continuous line. Traditionally they are all worked the same size; however, when the three elements of angle, length of stitch and position are changed, an organic random effect is created which I have used in this book to decorate raw edges and create shading.

**1** Two broken lines provide a guide for working random herringbone stitches in straight lines.

**2** Two wavy broken lines show herringbone stitches worked in wavy lines and overlapping rows as in Project 6 'Butterflies in a box'.

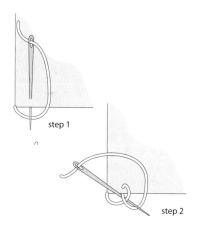

**insertion: knotted buttonhole stitch**

**Steps 1 and 2** Two buttonhole stitches are worked approximately 4 mm ($\frac{3}{16}$ in) apart on the two edges to be joined to create the 'knots' .

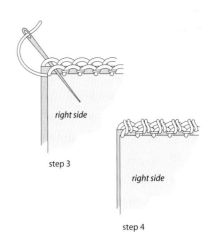

step 3

right side

right side

step 4

**Steps 3 and 4** Hold the two buttonholed edges together, right sides facing out, and wrap twice over and through each loop. The loops may not always be opposite each other and may be whipped once or twice as their relative positions dictate.

## knot, half-hitch

Half-hitch, a term used of a knot, is the same as a buttonhole stitch. See also the instructions for wrapped and beaded cords and for continuous cords. Make a loop in front and behind the core and on top of the loop and tighten.

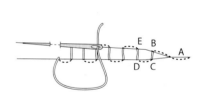

## knot, overhand

1 Place the right end of the yarn over and under the left end of the yarn to form a loop.
2 The same knot made on a cord.
3 The same knot made with two cords.

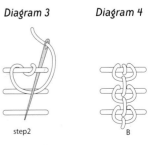

1      2      3

## ladder stitch

Worked with matching sewing cotton in an embroidery needle, ladder stitch is ideal for joining two edges together without the stitches showing. The needle enters the fold of the fabric exactly opposite, making vertical stitches between B-C, D-E, etc.

## raised chain band

Work the required number of horizontal straight stitch bars in medium weight thread such as perle 5 or 8, approximately 1 cm (⅜ in) wide. A curved line of raised chain band is made by radiating the bars evenly around a curve.
**Diagram 1** Bring needle and thread out at A, above and at the centre of the bar.
**Step 1** Push the needle from south to north on the left of A, under the bar, and pull the thread with medium to firm tension, ntf.
**Diagram 2** Tension is always made on step 1.
**Diagram 3,** Step 2 Make a semi-circular loop of thread and push the needle from north to south on the right of A, under the bar and above the loop, ntf. Pull this looped chain loosely as it will be tensioned in step 1 of the next stitch
**Diagram 4** Repeat step 1 again and pull the tension so that the previous looped chain stitch is rounded with medium tension. Repeat steps 1 and 2 to the end of the bars and finish off the thread through the fabric and at the back of the work at B.

*Diagram 1*          *Diagram 2*

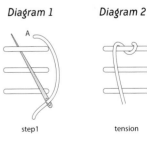

step1          tension

*Diagram 3*          *Diagram 4*

step2          B

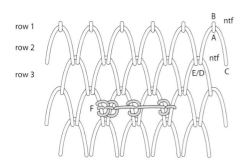

row 1
row 2
row 3

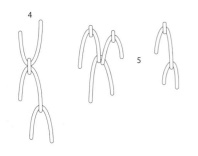

4

5

## raised chain band and wave stitch

Wave stitch is worked first as follows:

**Row 1** The first row is a line of vertical straight stitches, A-B.

**Row 2** The second row consists of stitches resembling inverted V shapes, C-D, each stitch threaded through a vertical stitch made in the first row.

**Row 3** The third and subsequent rows of stitches are threaded behind one arm each of two stitches in the previous row, D-E, and do not pass through the fabric. Continue working rows backwards and forwards, varying the distance between rows and the length and number of stitches in each row

**4** Two directions may be worked from one vertical straight stitch.

**5** Add more wave stitches in isolated groups by commencing with one ore more vertical straight stitches.

Work raised chain band on top of the wave stitches, turning the work sideways so that the wave stitches are made on horizontal bars, F in row 3.

## raised chain band, **multiples**

Work two or three raised chains on each or every second bar.

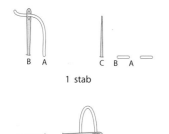

## running stitch

One of the most versatile stitches in embroidery, running stitch is explored in many of the projects in this book.

**1** Running stitch by the stab-stitch method.

**2** Running stitch by the scoop method.

**3** Running stitch with medium tension.

**4** Running stitch with tight tension. When working running stitch in horizontal rows with tight tension, the stitches push the fabric in the spaces between the stitches upward to create hills and ridges.

1 stab

2 scoop

*Right: running stitch with medium tension; **far right**: running stitch by the scoop method*

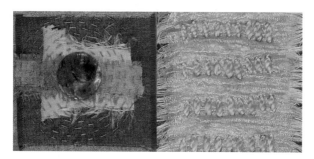

## slip stitch

Used for hems and attaching linings.

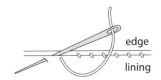

## straight stitch

Although simple, straight stitches convey mood, movement and direction, varied by their length, thickness and placement.

1 Straight stitch, diagonal, worked horizontally left to right or vertically top down.
2 Vertical straight stitch, worked horizontally left to right, or vertically top down.
3 Scattered straight stitches.
4 Tight tension: When straight stitches spaced approximately 6 mm (¼ in) apart are worked with tight tension in vertical rows from the top down they push the fabric downwards in the spaces between the rows, creating valleys as shown in the detail from Project 4 'Gift wrap'. Each row must be started at the top and secured at the end of each vertical row to hold the tension and create the effect.

## vandyke stitch

This lovely textured stitch can be worked on the surface of the fabric or used to make a dramatic impact worked over cords or thread padding in straight or wavy lines.

A vertical straight stitch, A-B, is made to start. The first stitch is made by coming out at C, crossing to the right and taking needle and thread through the loop A-B, ntf, crossing over to the right and down into D. Subsequent stitches are made the same way but passing the needle and thread behind the previous stitch as shown by the position of the needle behind the loop E-F. The width of the arms may be equal or unequal.

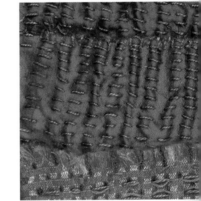

## vandyke stitch, **overstitched on cord**

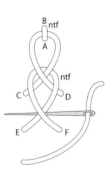

## wave stitch

See instructions above for raised chain band and wave stitch combined.

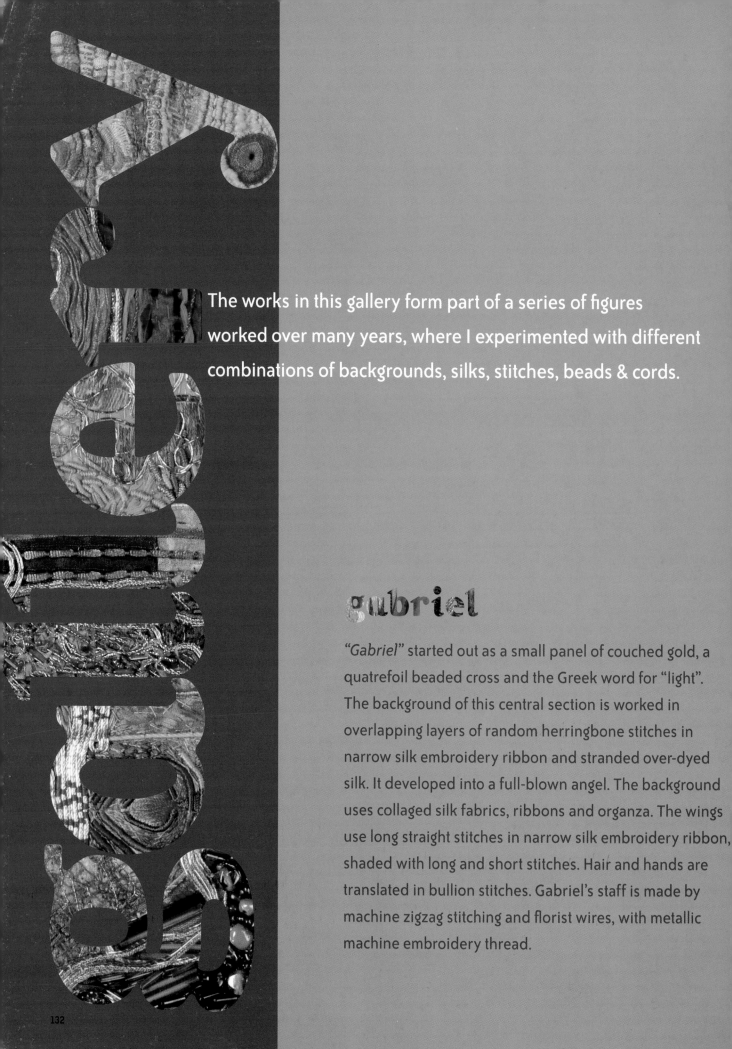

**gallery**

The works in this gallery form part of a series of figures worked over many years, where I experimented with different combinations of backgrounds, silks, stitches, beads & cords.

## gabriel

*"Gabriel"* started out as a small panel of couched gold, a quatrefoil beaded cross and the Greek word for "light". The background of this central section is worked in overlapping layers of random herringbone stitches in narrow silk embroidery ribbon and stranded over-dyed silk. It developed into a full-blown angel. The background uses collaged silk fabrics, ribbons and organza. The wings use long straight stitches in narrow silk embroidery ribbon, shaded with long and short stitches. Hair and hands are translated in bullion stitches. Gabriel's staff is made by machine zigzag stitching and florist wires, with metallic machine embroidery thread.

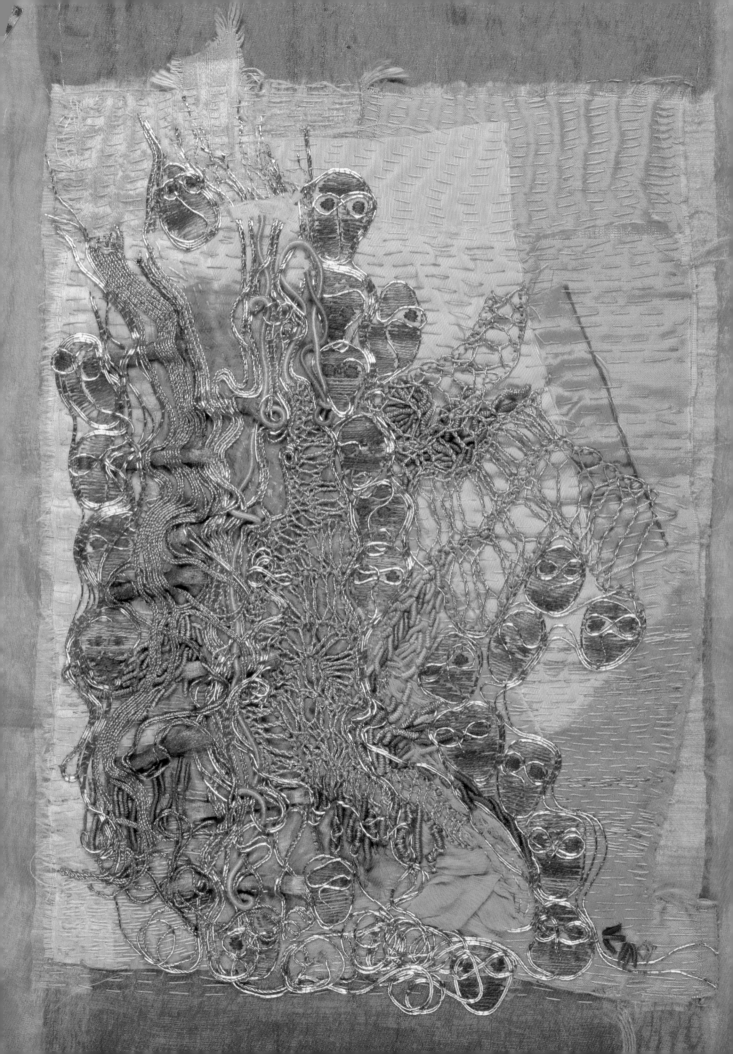

# ghosts of kurnell

*"Ghosts of Kurnell"* (opposite) explores ripples of raised, couched gold threads, detached Breton stitch, continuous cords and running stitch undulations. The "ghosts" appeared in a series of photos taken of sacred rocks and sea water.

# byzantine angel

*"Byzantine Angel"* (page 136) endeavours to capture the richness of a Byzantine icon, with collaged silk background sponged with gold paint, couched metal threads, beads, blanket, herringbone and long and short stitches, and soft buttonholed rings for ringlets of hair.

# grief angel

*"Grief Angel"* (page 137) explores background collage and merging, fabric manipulation and metal threads, using long and short stitch and soft buttonholed rings for ringlets of hair.

# aphrodite

*"Aphrodite"* features the discovery of
'chopped silk'. It uses collaged silk background,
couched metal threads, chopped silk (dress),
and bullion stitches.

# nature strip

*"Nature Strip"* (work in progress) investigates stitch tension, colour and wrapping, worked in the hand. There are buttonhole and bullion stitches, blanket two rows wrapped together, continuous cords. The two rows of blanket stitch were worked with very tight tension to create undulations of fabric, and then wrapped one, two or more times with different types of thread.

# references

Butler, Anne, *Embroidery Stitches*, Batsford, London, 1979 (fancy hem stitch)

Pesel, Louisa F., *Stitches from Eastern Embroideries* Percy Lund Humphries, London, 1912/1913
(Origins: Portugal, Crete, Hispano-Moresque) (herringbone and overlapping herringbone stitch)

John, Edith, *Creative Stitches*, Dover, 1967 (linked bullions)

Enthoven, Jacqueline, *The Stitches of Creative Embroidery*, Van Nostrand, Reinhold, New York, 1964
(chained cross stitch)

# suppliers Australia & overseas

## threads silk, cotton and metallic, and silk embroidery ribbon

Barnyarns (Ripon) Ltd
Canal Wharf
Bondgate Green
Ripon North Yorkshire HG4 1AQ
Tel: 01765 690069
www.barnyarns.co.uk
(Madeira threads and lots of
other things)

Cascade House Australia
86 Albert Street
Creswick Victoria 3363 Australia
Tel: 61 3 5345 1120
www.cascadehouse.com.au

Coats Craft UK
PO Box 22
McMullen Road
Darlington
Co. Durham DL1 1YQ
Tel: 01325 365457
www.coatscrafts.co.uk

Coats Australia Pty Ltd.
125 Station Road
Seven Hills NSW 2147 Australia
Tel: 61 2 9838 5200
and 1800 227 401

Colour Streams
5 Palm Ave
Mullumbimby NSW 2482 Australia
Tel: 61 2 66842577
(hand space-dyed silk threads,
embroidery ribbon and fabrics)
www.colourstreams.com.au and
info@colourstreams.com.au

DMC threads global
www.dmc.com

Gumnut Yarns
P.O. Box 858
Bathurst NSW 2795 Australia
Tel: 61 2 63326771
info@gumnutyarns.com

Madeira Australia
SSS Pty Limited
16–18 Valediction Road
Kings Park NSW 2148 Australia
Tel: 61 2 9672 3888
www.sewingcraft.com

Madeira Threads (UK) Ltd.
Thirst Industrial Park
York Road, Thirsk
North Yorkshire Y07 3BX
Tel: 01845 524880
www.madeira.co.uk

Madeira USA
www.madeirausa.com

Mulberry Silks, Patricia Wood
Silkwood
4 Park Close
Tetbury, Gloucestershire GL8 8HS
Tel: 01666 503438
www.mulberrysilks-patriciawood.com
(silk threads in a variety of weights –
lovely coordinated colour packs)

Oliver Twists
22 Phoenix Road
Crowther
Washington, Tyne and Wear
NE38 0AD
Tel: 0191 4166016
(threads, metal shim, wires, etc.)
(no website)

Ristal Threads
4 Hercules Street
Murrumbateman NSW 2582
Australia
Tel: 61 2 6226 8200
info@ristalthreads.com

Stef Francis
Waverley, Higher Rocombe, Stoke in Teignhead
Newton Abbot, Devon TQ12 4QL
Tel: 01803 323004
www.stef-francis.co.uk
(hand-dyed threads, fabrics, etc.)

Texere Threads
College Mills
Barkerend Road, Bradford BD3 9AQ
Tel: 01274 722191
www.texere.co.uk

The Silk Route
32 Wolseley Road
Godalming, Surrey GU7 3EA
Tel: 01666 840881

21st Century Yarns
Unit 18, Langston Priory
Kingham, Oxfordshire OX7 6UP
www.21stcenturyyarns.com
(hand-dyed fabrics and threads)

Metallic threads
Benton and Johnson
Regalia House
Newtown Road
Bedworth, Warwickshire CV12 8QR
www.bentonandjohnson.com

Golden Hinde
28 Edward Gardens
Warrington WA1 4QT
Tel: 01925 810697.
www.golden-hinde.co.uk
(goldwork supplies and metal threads)

Golden Threads
Brimstone Cottage
Pounsley, Blackboys, Uckfield TN22 5HS
Tel: 01825 831815
www.goldenthreads.co.uk
(gold threads, etc.)

**fabrics** silk fabrics and organza from general fabric, wedding and after five stores;
Indian muslin from general fabric stores

Borovicks Fabric Ltd
16 Berwick Street
London W1V 4HP
Tel: 020-7437-2180/0520
www.borovicksfabric.co.uk

Rainbow Silks
27 New Road
Amersham, Bucks HP6 6KD
Tel: 01494 727003

The Silk Route
Cross Cottage
Cross Lane
Frimley Green, Surrey GU16 6LN
Tel: 01252 835781
www.thesilkroute.co.uk
(all sorts of silk fabrics)

Whaleys (Bradford) Ltd.
Harris Court
Great Horton
Bradford, West Yorkshire BD7 4EQ
Tel: 01274 567718
www.whaleys-bradford.ltd.co.uk
(muslin and other fabrics)

Winifred Cottage
17 Elms Road
Fleet, Hampshire GU51 3EG
Tel: 01252 617667
www.winifredcottage.co.uk
(lots of threads, dissolvable fabrics, chiffon scarves, etc.)

Embroiderers' Guild
PO Box 42B
East Molesey KT8 9BB
Tel: 0181 943 1229
(The World of Embroidery and Stitch magazines, which list up-to-date suppliers)

# beads and cords; handcraft and jewellery suppliers

Art Van Go
The Studios
1 Stevenage Road
Knebworth, Herts SG3 6AN
Tel: 01438 814946
www.artvango.co.uk
(all sorts of art materials, gels,
multimedia stuff)

Fine-tipped soldering irons, acrylic
felt, nylon organza, paper nylon and
PVC fabric are all available by mail
order from
Margaret Beal
Tel: 01264 365102
Email: burningissues@margaretbeal.
co.uk

Craftynotions Ltd
Unit 2 Jessop Way
Newark NG24 2ER
Tel: 01636 700862
www.craftynotions.com
(charms, materials, paints, etc.)
Gallery Textiles
4a Canalside, Metal & Ores Industrial
Estate
Hanbury Road
Stoke Prior, Worcs B60 4JZ
Tel: 01527 882288. www.
gallerytextiles.co.uk
(lots of craft things – stamps, inks,
textile pens, etc.)

Nid-noi.com
126 Norwich Drive
Brighton, BN2 4LL
Tel: 01273 698112
www.nid-noi-com
(all sorts of stuff, including heavy-
weight pelmet Vilene – also known as
craft Vilene)

Stitch 'n' Craft
Swan's Yard,
High Street
Shaftsbury, Dorset SP7 8JQ
Tel: 01747 830666 (mail order),
01747 852500
www.stitchncraft.co.uk
(all sorts of equipment, beads, etc.)

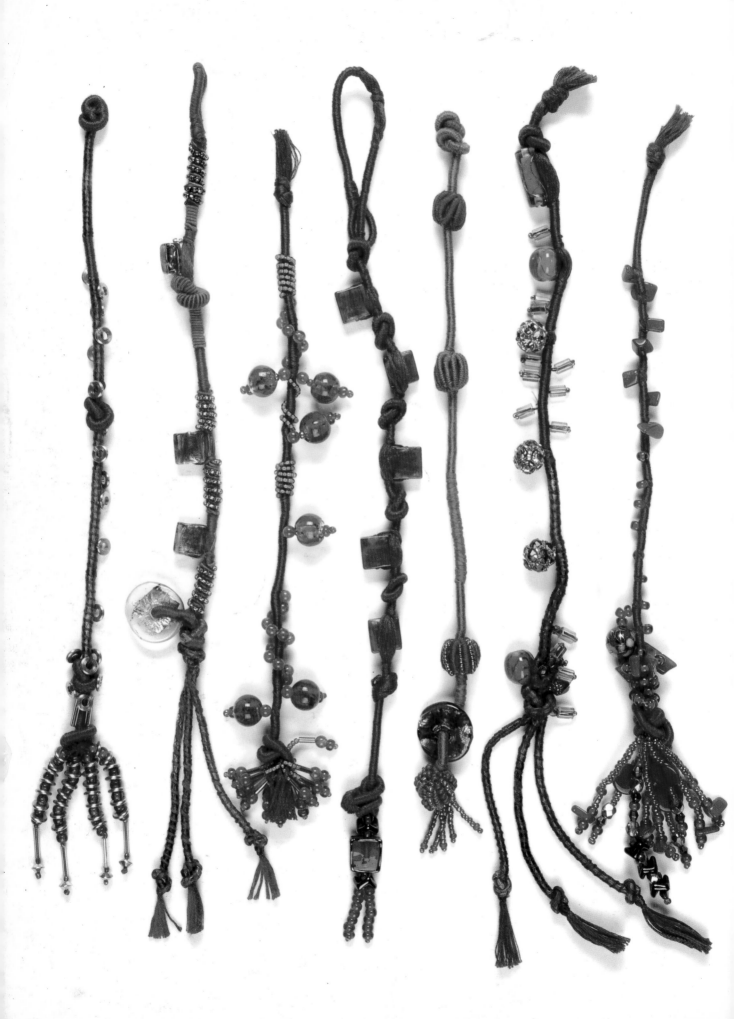